ITALIAN VILLAS

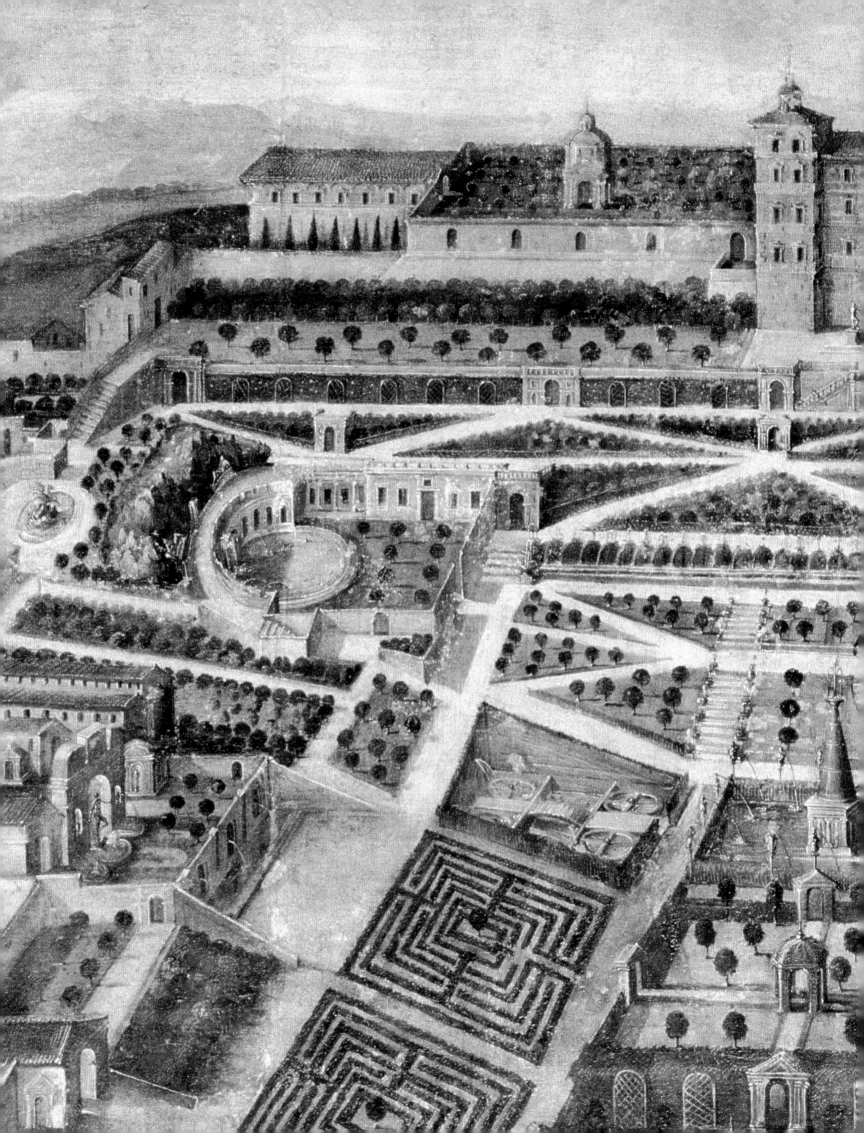

"It would be worthwhile siting the villa where the rays of the sun will trouble your eyes neither when you set out in the morning nor when you return in the evening. [. . .] On the other hand, anywhere too busy is to be avoided, as is anywhere next to a town, a military road, or a port that attracts many ships; the ideal location would be one that enjoys the benefits of the above, yet where your family life will not be plagued by visits from acquaintances who are passing by."

Leon Battista Alberti
(*On the Art of Building*, Book Five)

OVIDIO GUAITA

ITALIAN VILLAS

ABBEVILLE PRESS PUBLISHERS

NEW YORK   LONDON

First published in the United States of America
in 2003 by Abbeville Press, 116 West 23rd Street,
New York, N.Y. 10011

Original title: *La Villa in Italia* by Ovidio Guaita
First published in Italy in 2002 by
Bolis Edizioni srl, Italy
© 2002 Bolis Edizioni srl, Italy
English translation © 2003 Bolis Edizioni srl, Italy

Photographs: Ovidio Guaita
Graphic design and layout: Studio Priori & C., Milan
Art Director: Barbara Pedetta
English translation: Marguerite Shore

Library of Congress Cataloguing-in-Publication Data

Guaita, Ovidio
   [Villa in Italia. English]
   Italian Villas / text and photography by Ovidio Guaita.
      p. cm.
   Includes bibliographical references and index.
   ISBN 0-7892-0804-0 (alk.paper)
   1. Architecture, Domestic—Italy. I. Title.
NA7594.G7813 2003
728.8'0945—dc21
2003052061

First edition

9 8 7 6 5 4 3 2 1

ISBN: 0-7892-0804-0

ACKNOWLEDGMENTS

This book emerged from the author's work with the magazine *VilleGiardini* and was inspired by the editor there, Nani Prina, who directed and sometime accompanied Guaita on his journeys through the countryside. Some of the drawings were created by students in the seminars the author holds each year, as part of Fausia Farneti's art history course at the School of Architecture in Florence. The author's friend and colleague Lawrence Taylor worked with him on the organization and completion of on-site visits. Heartfelt thanks go to all these people.

Front cover: Palazzo del Te (Mantua)

Back cover: Villa Vimercati Sanseverino in Vaiano Cremasco (Cremona).

pages 2-3: Medici Villa of Camugliano (Pisa).

pages 4-5: Ceiling of the Hall of Giants, Palazzo del Te (Mantua).

pages 6-7: Villa Valguarnera, Bagheria (Palermo).

pages 8-9: Villa d'Este, Tivoli (Rome), painting by an anonymous 17th-century artist.

pages 10-11: Villa Barbaro, Maser (Treviso).

p. 12: Leon Battista Alberti, On the Art of Building in Ten Books, *translated by Joseph Rykwert, Neil Leach and Robert Tavernor, Cambridge, Mass., MIT Press, 1988. Reprinted with permission.*

Excerpts from Italian Journey *by Johann Wolfgang von Goethe, translation by W.H. Auden and Elizabeth Mayer. Reprinted with permission.*

CONTENTS

THE VILLA IN ITALY

A House for Leisure (Otium) and business (Negotium)

The villa, understood as the *locus amoenus*, or "pleasurable place," meant to provide intellectual leisure and healthy country living as well as a base for managing country properties, became a widespread phenomenon in certain regions of Italy beginning in the fifteenth century. This was really a revival; in Roman imperial times, between the first century B.C. and the first century A.D., the term *villa* already indicated a residence situated in the fields and tied to agricultural activity. In fact the word might refer to an elegant dwelling or to a group of rustic buildings meant to house farmworkers, in contrast to the *domus* or the palazzo, a single-family urban dwelling characterized by connections to the urban fabric. The *casa*, or cottage, was a simple dwelling outside the city. The term *villa* was generic and seldom used, though it took on a negative sense when it referred to so-called *villani,* or inhabitants of a villa.

"What news is there of Como, my delight and yours," wrote Pliny the Younger (A.D. 62–ca. 112) to his friend Caninius Rufus around A.D. 96, "and of that lovely suburban villa? that portico, where it is always Spring? that most shady grove of plane trees? and the green and crystalline canal? and the nearby lake that extends out and supplies it?" In *Epistle* 5.6.45, Pliny describes his villa in Tuscany: "I never feel as well, either intellectually or physically, as when I am there. In fact, I exercise my mind with literary concerns and my body with hunting. For my servants too, there is no place where they enjoy better health. . . . I only wish that in the future the Gods also might continue to grant such joy to me and such virtue to this place." The Roman villa opened up to the surrounding space and had porticoed courtyards, as well as patios that faced onto the landscape, terraces, baths, and peristyles that related the architecture to nature. This contact was essential for fulfilling its primary function as a place intended for meditation, contemplation, and convivial debate.

Twentieth-century reconstruction of the Villa dei Papiri in Herculaneum, which was buried beneath the eruption of Vesuvius in A.D. 79. Commissioned by American financier Paul Getty, it now houses the Getty Museum in Los Angeles, California.

THE REBIRTH OF HUMANISM

The villa again played a role in the era of humanism, with the rediscovery of the classical world, following its fall into oblivion in the Middle Ages. The Latin word *villa* was incorporated into the new Italian language and signified something like the original, but embellished with a "refined" emphasis. The agricultural-residential function that the original term expressed gained new implications; the formal values of the new buildings and their noble nature came to distinguish the villa typology from that of other agricultural buildings. These new dwellings were the product of a cultivated design; no longer the work of simple laborers, they showcased the creative ability of skilled architects. A new terminology emerged, in large part derived from rural buildings, to indicate the villa's many different forms in the various regions of Italy. For example, these new creations, always characterized and ennobled by the presence of the main dwelling and a more or less elaborate decorative scheme, are called

Fresco depicting a villa by the sea, found in a dwelling in Pompeii, where refined plays of perspectival illusion were developed.

cascine and *corti* in the Po Valley, *vigne* in Latium, *masserie* in Puglia, and *casene* and *bagli* in Sicily. The emblem of the transformation and opening up of medieval society, as well as the new humanistic ferment, the villa was, more than any other building, an offspring of humanism, of a renewed faith in man and nature, and of the rediscovery of the classical origins of our culture. But the spirit of emulation entailed new meanings and values; in contrast to the rough power represented by the castle, the villa presented a more enduring and unassailable magnificence. In the fifteenth century the villa also served to project the city's security into rural areas. Though it is difficult to say precisely how it contributed to this tranquillity, it conveyed an extremely clear message of ownership over the countryside.

THE VILLA TODAY

Today the word *villa* connotes a single-family dwelling of average-to-large dimensions. The word implies a refined design process, ennobled by decorations, coats of arms or paintings, and a location outside urban centers or their immediate vicinity, connected to surrounding nature by gardens and parks. It is precisely this relationship to nature—the way it establishes a dialogue through a surrounding area of planned greenery—that distinguishes the villa from the urban palace or the castle. In fact it represents the antithesis of the city, contrasting the virtues and pleasures of the countryside to the vices and excesses of city life. The villa's outbuildings, grouped together in different ways, reproduce a small court, the various

Imperial Rome had a strong tradition of seaside vacation villas, some of which are depicted in this fresco from Stabiae (Naples).

components structured according to precise hierarchies. With their geometric designs, the gardens that flank these dwellings also confirm the master's ability to control and rule.

The villa historically has assumed various functions. First of all, it has been a wholesome getaway for the owner, who generally lived in a city palace. A gentleman might have passed the holidays in the countryside, but often, particularly in the fifteenth and sixteenth centuries, he went there even more to oversee the important phases of his crops' growing cycle. Sometimes the villa was used exclusively as an official residence—with impressive drawing rooms that left little space for private life—or, more frequently, as a hunting lodge. Thus it has been a luxury accessory for the privileged classes. Paradoxically, it has been precisely this component of futility that has given free rein to the creativity of those who designed villas.

Fifteenth and Sixteenth Centuries

During the fifteenth century the first villas were built in the vicinity of large urban centers, as rural residences for the Renaissance courts, which used these buildings to assert their dominion over the countryside. In this period prominent figures in the worlds of trade and banking, with great sums of money to invest, viewed their landed estates and properties as a valid alternative to their primary activities.

The fifteenth and sixteenth centuries saw a notable development of the villa and garden typologies. Each was defined in increasing detail, and compositional solutions, materials, colors, and forms were embellished as never before. Beginning in the sixteenth century the experiences of humanism in Tuscany spread to varying degrees throughout the peninsula. Small centers of humanism where the new artistic and architectural language reached—such as Pienza, Mantua, Urbino, and Ferrara—continued these cities' traditions of magnificence, but without the hegemonic position they had held for a century.

Within this context Venice came to play a growing role. During this era Venice was moving its cultural center of gravity away from the east, turning increasingly to the fate of its territories on the mainland. The settling of the political situation favored the draining and apportioning of vast lands that soon proved to be fertile and thus an excellent investment. These extensive possessions came to the Venetians in various and sometimes dubious ways. Such appropriations did not pass unnoticed and were criticized both by authorities on the mainland—who saw their best lands taken away—and by those in Venice proper, who were

worried that less attention was being paid to maritime trade, the origin of the Republic's for-
tune. Nonetheless the Venetians continued to build sumptuous dwellings, using as their
architectural point of reference the work of the renowned Andrea Palladio.

MEDICI RULE

Meanwhile the Medici, lords of Florence, had become the most important landowners in
Tuscany, reorganizing the territory by modernizing the infrastructure of roads and by extensively redeveloping land. The villa, which had by now become the retreat par excellence,
served to flaunt the power, wealth, and culture acquired by the noble house and its numerous
court. Here, as early as the fifteenth century, the prestige derived from artistically prized
assets was used to consolidate power, which was celebrated by satisfying the patron's ambition. In this manner investment became "productive," improving the image of the landown-

Farming had a strong impact on ancient dwellings in Italy. The villa typology evolved in part from farming settlements such as Corte Cappelletta in Palidano (Mantua), now owned by the Mora family.

ers, introducing them to more exclusive social levels, and encouraging crucial contacts for
substantial international business transactions. While the area of Florence acted as a magnet,
other regions developed autonomously. The Medici had long held lands in the region around
Pisa, and by 1568 these covered some 84,000 acres (34,000 hectares). Here—as in the region
of Siena known for its wealthy merchants and landowners, headed by the Chigi and the Piccolomini, and in Lucca, also known for its trade and wealth—numerous rural dwellings were
built, seen as crowning manifestations of the landed investments of the patrician class.

ROME OF THE POPES

During this same period papal Rome saw tight competition between the nobility and the clerical class, which competed for cultural and economic supremacy as well as political power. Princes and cardinals vied to sponsor works of opulence and beauty and to engage the greatest architects, decorators, painters, and sculptors. The designers who worked in the city or passed through while involved in projects included Bartolommeo Ammannati, Gian Lorenzo Bernini, Francesco Borromini, Donato Bramante, Pirro Ligorio, Baldassarre Peruzzi, Giulio Romano, Giuliano da Sangallo, Raphael Sanzio, and Jacopo Vignola. Patrons wanted a grandiose stage for the pleasurable activities and events with which they entertained their courts. Their villas were erected amid the greenery of the towns closest to Rome, such as Tivoli and Frascati, or in the area of Viterbo, where, however, they were at the center of vast estates, and connected to populated areas such as in Caprarola, Bagnaia, or Bomarzo.

BIRTH OF A TYPOLOGY

Not until the fifteenth century was the villa presented as an organic unit, a complete project in the service of the pleasures and whims of man, who finally was achieving a serene relationship with his surroundings. At the same time the development of the villa in Tuscany was maturing. In particular, the Medici villas of Poggio a Caiano by Giuliano da Sangallo and Artimino by Bernardo Buontalenti, both located between Florence and Pistoia, constituted models of the country residence and were broadly imitated, even into the seventeenth century. Ambitious patrons used these places not only for official activities but also for their private pleasure. In fact, at the end of the sixteenth century the Medici and their entourage were usually in transit from villa to villa, an itinerant court in search of the best climate and following the phases of the hunt and agricultural activities. The delightful holiday spots set aside for their wanderings were ennobled by the "delights" that the Florentine family had built, beginning in the second half of the fifteenth century. First they transformed late-medieval buildings, such as Castello del Trebbio or Villa Cafaggiolo, and then they created completely new villas, such as those of Poggio a Caiano, Pratolino, Artimino, Lappaggi, and others.

In the rest of Tuscany, political insecurity and the subdivision of landed estates slowed down the establishment of villas until the first half of the sixteenth century. But with the advent of the Grand Duchy and the creation of numerous hydraulic systems to deal with

Opposite: The frescoed gallery on the second floor of the Villa Grazioli in Frascati (Rome). This painting cycle was commissioned by Cardinal Ottavio Acquaviva d'Aragona.

frequent flooding, the process of land division moved forward. At the same time, along with traditional grape and olive cultivation, grain and rice farming become more extensive. Medici architect Bernardo Buontalenti, the designer of various Florentine residences, also worked throughout the rest of the Grand Duchy, in the area of Pisa, for example, where he created the villa of Coltano. His influence soon spread to the region of Lucca, where his work functioned as a model.

Siena

When the Florentines arrived in Siena in the first half of the sixteenth century, after a long siege, the Sienese nobility realized that the renewed climate of détente and political stability was a blessing for the city's economy. Within a short time this sense of well-being was translated into a flowering of villas on the neighboring hillsides. The most prestigious were the work of Baldassarre Peruzzi, the architect favored by Agostino Chigi, the leading member of that noble family and an important figure in papal Rome. Vasari recounts that during the sack of Rome in 1527, the artist managed to flee to Siena, where he settled, building numerous residences. His presence decisively influenced his colleagues there, who also were inspired by his accomplishments in Rome. The result was the creation of a simple but equally expressive local style.

Lombardy

At the beginning of the seventeenth century, as the final echoes of Palladio's work died out and new stimuli arrived from Bernini's and Borromini's Rome, Baldassarre Longhena, a Venetian, was disseminating new villa and palazzo typologies, presaging the Baroque era. In nearby Lombardy, however, the villa was not yet as widespread a building type as in neighboring regions. This was due in part to the continuous movement of foreign armies through the region and in part to the plague of 1630, which decimated the population and generated a heavy economic recession. But the principal reason was the strength of the Counter-Reformation under Cardinal Carlo Borromeo, with his message of austerity. Nonetheless, the villa did take hold and flourish in Lombardy from the eighteenth century until the early decades of the twentieth century, particularly in the north, in the lake region, a favorite vacation spot for Italians and foreigners alike.

VILLAS, GARDENS, AND HOLIDAY RETREATS

Beginning in the eighteenth century, the relationship between villa and garden grew stronger. Architects and writers of treatises explored new expressive possibilities and attempted to codify earlier developments. One scholar in particular, Ottavio Bertotti Scamozzi, devoted himself to the rediscovery of Palladio's work, helping to consolidate the preeminent position of the architect from Vicenzo. During this period so-called Palladianism spread in the form of a rediscovery and imitation of the master's style. However the true sustainer of the "villa culture" begun by Palladio was the architect Francesco Muttoni, who worked almost exclusively in Vicenza, where he became known as the "little Palladio of the eighteenth century." While Baroque expressions were evolving, the eighteenth century witnessed a return to Palladian classicism. The villa typology grew increasingly complex and monumental, while interiors

The long neoclassical facade of the Villa Olmo in Como, built it in 1782 for Innocenzo Odescalchi by architect Innocenzo Regazzoni.

were decorated with refined polychrome stuccowork with floral motifs, landscapes, and chinoiserie, particularly at the hand of Giambattista Tiepolo and his disciples. In 1797, when the last doge was removed from office, the culture of the villa was still flourishing, and it would survive, if only by a short time, the now inexorable decline of the Venetian Republic.

Not everyone shared in this passion for the villa. In his preface to *Le smanie della villeggiatura* (roughly translated *Holiday Frenzy*) Carlo Goldoni complains, "Vacationers bring the pomp and tumult of the city into the countryside and have poisoned the pleasures of the peasants and the shepherds, who acquire their misery from the arrogance of their masters." The effects of eighteenth-century decadence were being felt, and the brutal exploitation of the land provoked a slow but constant decline in production that, coupled with the loss of a monopoly in trade, made economic depression inevitable.

EPICENTERS OF THE GRAND SIÈCLE

Thus the epicenters of the villa phenomenon shifted from the Veneto to Lombardy, which saw an increase in fine examples during this period. The great medieval estates were divided, while the ranks of the nobility were swelled by officials and military figures rewarded for their loyalty to the empire. The economic revival that characterized the period gave new life to the arts.

In Tuscany the situation was much the same. With the arrival of the Lorrainese, greater attention was given to the territory of the Grand Duchy, with the result that the villa style

The Villa di Oreno in Monza. This detailed eighteenth-century engraving by Marc'Antonio Dal Re is typical of representations commissioned from artists during this period by the owners of such dwellings.

spread beyond Florence to other centers. In Pistoia, for example, numerous lovely vacation residences were built. The Panciatichi, the Gatteschi, the Forteguerri, and other powerful families from Pistoia used these dwellings as garrisons for their immense property investments, living there almost exclusively during the harvest season to escape the oppressive city heat and the "constriction" of their urban palaces. While Rome and Latium now basked in the reflected glory of the opulence of the sixteenth and seventeenth centuries, in Naples fashionable holiday dwellings sprang up on the slopes of Vesuvius, where two typologies took form. The first (and more ancient) emphasized the productive aspect of the land, in villa-farmhouses, comfortable but clearly not in step with worldly pleasures. The main building in these had numerous openings onto the best view and a large rustic courtyard with related outbuildings. The courtyard typically had blind arches, galleries supported by small barrel vaults, and various large corbels that emphasized the principal elements. In the eighteenth century a second typology developed; designed specifically as vacation houses, these were "places of delight." In many cases renovations of older and more spartan weekend residences for the most part along the coast, they were notable for their refined elegance. The principal body of the structure, several stories high, faced onto the public road, and two side wings, articulated in various ways, enclosed an open court looking toward a garden. A single axis of symmetry crossed the entire property, sometimes continuing beyond the road. In that case, the entrance on the house's principal façade would be paired with another at the entrance to the property, which gave access onto the fields.

PALERMO AND BAGHERIA

The eighteenth century was the age of the vacation house par excellence, and these were situated in the most beautiful parts of the peninsula. In a continuous competition for luxury and exhibition, the Italian gentry squandered fabulous fortunes, and one of the areas they particularly coveted was the Conca d'Oro, favored by the Sicilian aristocracy. Residences there were inhabited for half the year, and the nobility would move there in long caravans, made up of an entire court of friends, women, knights, pages, and servants. Time at the villa was spent in chivalrous games, interminable shooting parties, and enormous meals. Throughout the seventeenth century Palermo preserved a fortified military layout, and expansion beyond the city was still modest. But the suffocating city no longer suited the exuberant nobility, which wanted to exhibit its culture and above all its wealth in the form of new residences. These catered to a more relaxed lifestyle, within nature a "natural" setting tamed with precise geometry in fragrant gardens. The city expanded in three directions: Bagheria, Monreale, and Piana dei Colli. The villas of Palermo—unlike those in the Veneto, for example, which had a symbiotic relationship with the surrounding nature—developed and updated the "male" idea of the small fortress, reflecting a closed and egocentric baronial culture that was in some ways still feudal. Generally the dwelling consisted of a two-story linear building element with lower service wings for servants' quarters and stables, arranged in a U shape. The facades were rigidly symmetrical, framed by pilaster strips, bands, cornices, and friezes in yellow tufa, like theatrical backdrops dominated by chiaroscuro effects—made to be seen more than experienced or touched. The exclusive Palermitan residence is characterized not by courtyards but by monumental exterior axial staircases. These vary in form but share a symmetrical double flight of stairs that describe elegant movements in space but often remain extraneous to the facade, while constituting its preeminent theatrical motif.

In Sicily, eighteenth-century landowners usually received their subjects in the courtyard in front of the building, using this physical separation to emphasize distinctions in rank. The villas of the Grand Siècle bear witness to this aristocratic isolation of the nobles and their alienation from everyday life. In many ways this century saw a heightening of themes developed earlier, such as the panoramic view. Achieving such views entailed cutting through miles of countryside, creating a new territorial sense of order. The keynotes were a theatrical setting, increasingly mined for all its possibilities; formal refinement, which now hinged on bold, virtuosic compositional effects; and above all unusual size.

DECLINE

The influence of the French grandeur of Fontainebleau and Versailles greatly expanded the scale on which gardens were created. These now involved entire towns, as in the case of the Villa Reale at Caserta or the Villa Pisani in Stra. In 1726 Marc'Antonio Dal Re published his first collection of engravings, entitled *Ville di delizia o siano palagi camparecci nello Stato di Milano*, which showed the most interesting and grand Lombard creations in bird's-eye view. Thus a single glance could take in the complex vastness of these villas and gardens. Terraces, avenues arranged in diagonal and sunburst configurations, citrus orchards, fountains, pools, and arabesqued garden *parterres* were celebrated in all their splendor and magnificence. But the advent of the industrial revolution gradually destroyed the economic base on which villa life was founded. The spread of the middle class shattered the financial dominance of patrons, and the newly rich could no longer afford to build and maintain these sumptuous monuments to personal power, wealth, and culture. Villas became increasingly modest in size and unassuming in their decorative apparatus until, in the nineteenth century, the term *villino* was coined to describe an elegant bourgeois residence that was only a shadow of the villa of the past.

Opposite: The neoclassical facade of the Villa Spedalotto in Bagheria (Palermo). The dwelling stands on a hill, next to the public road; an olive grove still surrounds it.

Goethe

From a bourgeois family, son of an imperial official, Johann Wolfgang von Goethe first studied law in Leipzig before devoting himself to literature, poetry, dramaturgy, and painting. He returned to Frankfurt for health reasons and then, in 1770, moved to Strasbourg, where he continued his studies, devoting himself to music, art, anatomy, and chemistry. During this period he formed friendships that would be fundamental for his development as a man and an author. He remained in the capital city of Alsace until 1775, writing famous novels such as *The Sorrows of Young Werther* and the first version of *Faust*.

Goethe then moved to Weimar to work as a tutor to the duke of that city, who was then barely eighteen years old. He remained there for ten years, leaving for a journey to Italy in 1786 to distance himself from court life, which had become too restrictive for him, and to seek new sources of inspiration for his work. He first visited the major cities in northern Italy, then went to Sicily and Naples. Finally he settled in Rome, where he stayed until 1788. While there he studied art and classical architecture, as the Renaissance artists had done, and in Rome he sensed that he had arrived at the source of his inspiration, the origins of his culture, a place where he felt authentic and genuine passion. His entire journey, which included a return home and a second Roman sojourn, is documented in his book *Italian Journey*, not published until many years later, in 1816 and 1829—a detailed record of Goethe's encounters, visits, impressions, and descriptions. This testi-

mony offers us not only an image of specific buildings toward the end of the eighteenth century but, reading between the lines, a window on the artistic atmosphere and sensibility of people of culture of the time. *Italian Journey* is also an important document for the history of many Italian villas, given Goethe's passion for architecture. This book quotes Goethe on numerous occasions, perhaps not always as an objective observer, but sometimes as the only witness or in any case the most reliable among those available.

A nineteenth-century view of Sorrento as Goethe saw it, and as he would have presented it to his readers.

THE NORTHWEST

PIEDMONT

LIGURIA

LOMBARDY

PIEDMONT

Gardens and "Vessels"

Long a theater of territorial disputes between various property owners, the Piedmont region is dotted with castles. These sometimes are considerable in size, but always with a defensive as well as residential purpose. Only in the seventeenth

homes, and foundation headquarters. Nonetheless their presence continues to offer solace to a sojourn on the lakeshore, as they bear witness to an enduring tradition of refined hospitality.

The beauty of Lake Verbano's shores was

Below: Engraving by Marc'Antonio Dal Re, depicting Isola Bella in Stresa (Novara), on Lake Maggiore.

and eighteenth centuries, with the rise of vacation houses, did true villas begin to be built, particularly on the lakeshores.

A notable number and variety of elegant and noble residences overlook Lake Maggiore, and beautiful and particularly charming gardens surround them, although many of these complexes now have become hotels, museums, retirement

extolled in the past, but for many centuries these were populated only by small groups of fishermen housed in cabins at the water's edge. But in the second half of the sixteenth century, at the height of the Renaissance, when the territory's boundaries were secure and the local economy stable, the Borromeo family arrived from Milan. One of the foremost families in Lombardy, they owned the

Opposite: The so-called Massimo Theater in the garden of Isola Bella.

Pages 32–33: Ceiling of the atrium of the Villa Imperiale Scassi in Genoa, with a representation of Samson felling the wild beast, commissioned by Gian Vincenzo Imperiale.

Opposite: Palazzo Borromeo on Isola Madre, Stresa.

Below: View of Isola Bella, Stresa.

building and garden complexes of Isola Bella and Isola Madre. These two islands are still intact, due to a fortunate coincidence of interests, geographic conditions, and the cultural background of their mentors. Giulio Cesare Borromeo called Isola Bella a "fantastic flowered vessel, stopped on the waters of the lake," a vessel with a Baroque cast, but one that still enchants even the most jaded

visitors with its beauty. Panoramic views and illusions compete to form a gigantic stage set, a grand backdrop for the staging of everyday life.

Thus amid gardens and vessels, centuries of history and architecture have passed by on the placid waters of Verbano, confirming how strong and deeply rooted the concept of the vacation house has been since the sixteenth century.

LAKE MAGGIORE

Opposite, right:
A corner of the garden
of Isola Bella.

Below and opposite, left:
Villa Ducale, Stresa, and
drawing of the facade.

Isola Bella assumed its current appearance thanks to Giulio Cesare Borromeo, better known as Carlo III, who began work there in 1620. The project was continued by Vitaliano VI, who described the island in detail before work began: "Previously this island was a rough cliff inhabited by fifty families, in rustic houses, most of them working as fishermen; and the cliff arose in the part looking southward in the shape of a mountain that then sloped downward somewhat toward the northwest."

This irregular and asymmetrical fishing village still exists, in piquant contrast to the rigid symmetry of the palace and garden. The main house is T-shaped, with a large drawing room at its center. The garden extends at the back, rigidly geometric and dominated by a fantastical stage set (the "Garden of Love") made up of statues, spires, and vases on walls covered in sponge stone and

shells. Vitaliano VI described it in 1677, on the occasion of the marriage of Carlo IV Borromeo and Giovanna Odescalchi: "On the side of the pyramid facing north, as it wasn't capable of citrus cultivation, and also to give variety, a theatrical perspective was shaped, two hundred Roman spans long and proportionately high, all composed of red granite, worked and well designed with large niches and mosaics, balustrades and

borders in soft *cieppo*; and forty statues. And at the summit there is a large niche with red granite and above a large rim of box trees; and in there is a statue that represents Lake Maggiore."

At the back, facing Stresa, a composition of flowerbeds and citrus trees was arranged specifically to be seen from the shore of the lake. Toward the end of the seventeenth century the complex was inhabited, if not completed, and was already called Isola Bella, in honor of Carlo III's wife, Isabella d'Adda.

Work and finishing touches continued in the decades that followed, but certain elements of the original design, such as a conspicuous wharf, were never built. Although the construction of the residence and the garden continued for a century, it looks like a unified project; nature has been disciplined into a preestablished form, thus celebrating the myth of man victorious over the natural elements, which he can tame at his pleasure. Rulers and powerful figures from through-

Villa Taranto, Pallanza (Novara); the garden (above) and back view of the building (right).

out Europe came to visit, curious to see such splendor; they included Napoleon, Carlo Felice of Savoy, Empress Alexandra Feodorovna of Russia, and Prince Charles of England.

The bizarre idea of constructing a villa on a small rocky island—later called Isola Madre, as it was the largest and the first to hold a noble residence—came suddenly to Lancellotto Borromeo, who was also a member of the powerful Borromeo family. In the early sixteenth century the ancient chapel of San Vittore stood on the cliff; at the time it was still in use, having been granted in perpetuity to the Borromeo family along with the neighboring lands. The family later obtained authorization to demolish it, to create a "sumptuous palace" embellished "with a charming garden," on the condition that the chapel would be rebuilt on the adjacent island.

This was the genesis of a place where, as Flaubert enthused, "nature lures you with a thousand strange seductions, you feel as if you are in an extremely sensual, extremely exquisite state."

The villa stood at the island's highest point, while the garden sloped down onto terraces oriented southward. There were two approaches: from the north, the most important, a staircase rose to the square in front of the house; the other, more to the south, linked to the terrace at the back, where the family sepulchral chapel, built by Count Vitaliano in 1858, also stood.

Oleander, agave, mimosa, palms, and eucalyptus flourished in the garden, along complex path-

ways wonderfully described by Carlo Amoretti in the early nineteenth century, in his *Viaggio da Milano ai tre laghi Maggiore, di Lugano e di Como e ne' monti che li circondano*: "To the south and east are five long trellised gardens, groves, and pergolas of citrus; to the north and west is a large wood of ancient and lofty laurel, fir trees, cypress, and broad evergreens, surrounded from place to place by vines. . . . The wood is populated with many pheasants and Numidia hens, which stay there because they have a comfortable and free existence, and because they don't have sufficient strength to fly as far as the opposite shore."

The ideal pursued by those building villas is

always that celebrated by Leon Battista Alberti nearly four centuries earlier: the marriage between *otium* and *negotium*, the pleasure of the elitist vacation home joined with the ability simultaneously to manage investments in the area. This concept remained more or less unchanged until the late eighteenth century, when an entrepreneurial aristocracy and an urban industrial bourgeoisie were on the rise, the members of which enjoyed the mere pleasure of staying at these places. During this period a building revival flourished along these shores, creating pleasurable retreats dedicated to the leisure of wealthy citizens.

The Garden of Love (left) and the garden in front of the Palazzo Borromeo, Isola Bella (above).

"When, by chance, someone has a heart and a shirt, he should sell his shirt in order to visit the area around Lake Maggiore," Stendhal wrote; and after him many other travelers extolled the lake's charms, contributing to its fame. The sixteenth-century residence commissioned by the Borromeo family was followed for the most part although they shared a desire for a view of the lake. However, they are characterized by neoclassical loggias, balconies, and turreted lookouts, which confirm the "open" character of these dwellings; their stylistic repertory is varied and eclectic, with neo-Gothic revivals, for example.

One of the most renowned of these creations

An elevation of the nineteenth-century Villa Pallavicino (right); the rear view of the villa (opposite), with Lake Maggiore in the background.

by modest palaces built in the small fishing villages at the initiative of the local patrician class. Not until the nineteenth century did grand neoclassical villas surrounded by dense parks, far from towns, begin to appear.

In the late nineteenth century the towns of Meina, Lesa, and Beligirate were described in the guide *Per laghi e monti* by Luigi Boniforti (1892) as an "orderly series of elegant dwellings whose beautiful facades are mirrored in the lake, where the waves bathe the grassy carpets and sloping steps of the superb gardens." These new settlements were never a true recurring typology,

is the Villa Pallavicino in Stresa. In 1855 a modest dwelling was built on the site, which was soon acquired by Marchese Ludovico Pallavicino of Genoa, who expanded both the house and the park. In 1864 the Genovese sculptor Carlo Rubatto was commissioned to create four medallions with busts of Ludovico Ariosto, Giovanni Boccaccio, Dante, and Petrarch on the entrance facing the hillside.

This residence stands out as one of the most significant examples of nineteenth-century holiday houses on Lake Verbano. Since the villa stands midway along the coast, the owner had to

build a road that linked it to both the public road below and the hillside above, so that the entire surrounding park could be crossed with ease.

The Villa Taranto in Pallanza is another very well known nineteenth-century dwelling. Its park is now even more renowned than the villa, which is the property of the Italian government and used as a conference site. The parkland is one of the most beautiful and varied along Lake Maggiore. It was created beginning in 1931 by Neil McEacharn, a

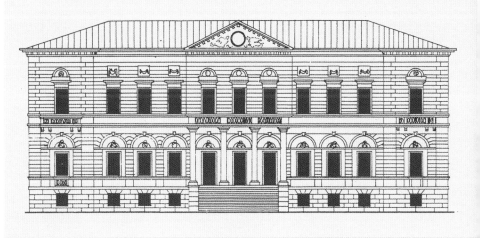

Scottish captain who acquired the property, naming it in honor of an ancestor who had been granted the title of duke of Taranto by Napoleon. The captain later promoted an ambitious program to organize the gardens, introducing a notable quantity of plants, particularly exotic varieties; the resulting botanical collection is of both great charm and significant scientific interest.

Today the grounds combine the geometric rigidity of the Italian-style garden with the sinuous "natural" volutes of a Romantic park, resulting in a unique environment that is one of most visited on the lake.

Above: The long neoclassical facade of the Villa Faraggiana, Maina (Novara); opposite, the facade today, overlooking a large garden.

LIGURIA

Between Land and Sea

The sixteenth century represents the most important era for the history of the villa in Liguria. This period saw the development and consolidation of the economic and political position of the city's patrician class, which controlled the entire region. A leading role was played by the cultivated patron Andrea Doria, who began work on his villa in Fas-

Sangallo the Younger. Fifteenth-century dwellings, which were asymmetrical, with decentralized entryways and L-shaped plans dominated by a predominantly horizontal development, were revolutionized. Large gardens and parks accompanied the new delights of holiday retreats, now disconnected from agricultural production and increas-

solo in 1528. In Genoa, the sixteenth-century art world was dominated by the strong personality of Galeazzo Alessi, an architect from Perugia. His decisive and innovative style helped to promulgate a new villa typology, characterized by a compact and monumental arrangement of volumes, embellished by a complex, plastic decorative scheme made up of architectural orders and large projecting cornices, inspired by earlier work in Rome by Donato Bramante and Antonio da

ingly isolated, intended for leisure activities and the "public relations" of the Genovese aristocracy.

Andrea Doria, leading patron, and Galeazzo Alessi, refined architect, made a decisive contribution to the artistic ascent of Renaissance Liguria. The sixteenth century was clearly the most fertile, but the periods that followed were also characterized by original expressive motifs that were mannered, yet always fascinating for the way they related to the environment.

Opposite: Aerial view of the garden of the Villa Pallavicini, in the Pegli quarter of Genoa; above, the Temple of Diana.

Andrea Doria

Oneglia, 1466–Genoa, 1560

The Genovese admiral Andrea Doria was a leading figure in the political life of Genoa, as well as one of the architects of the restoration of the Republic. From a young age, he served at various courts in Italy (Rome, Urbino, Naples) and Europe (Paris)—a typical background during the Renaissance for those destined to command

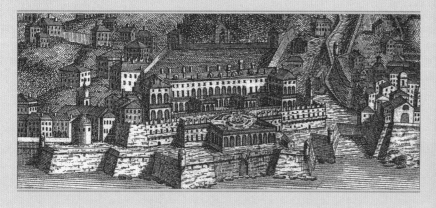

Above: Giovanni Lorenzo Guidotti, The Villa Doria, eighteenth-century engraving.

Right: Villa Doria Pamphili, Genoa.

and lead important families. Upon his return to Genoa, dismayed by the capital's cultural backwardness, he invited numerous well-known artists to the city to work on public buildings and, especially, on his own properties. From 1512 to 1522 he commanded the Genovese fleet, where he was distinguished for his courage. He then briefly served the French before aligning himself with Charles V and contributing to the restoration of the Republic in 1528. The emperor granted Doria special privileges as a prison contractor, which made him extremely wealthy. It was during this period that he began the

transformation of his villa in Fassolo, turning it into a sumptuous, princely dwelling. His wealth and splendor were such that the prince was able to compete with the Republic, offering better hospitality to important guests, such as Charles V himself (in 1533) and Philip II (in 1548).

Doria also was a skillful negotiator, obtaining favorable terms for fellow townsmen merchants who were doing business with Spain. He distinguished himself in the military arena in 1532, for the conquest of Patras in southern Greece, which was occupied by the Turks, and for saving the life of Charles V during an unsuccessful expedition to Algeria in 1541.

GENOA

The Villa Imperiale di Sant'Angelo, one of the first great Genovese villas, was built at Terralba toward the end of the fifteenth century, set into the greenery along the ancient Roman road. It was commissioned by Lorenzo Cattaneo, a rising nobleman from the finest aristocratic lines. Indeed when the villa was first opened in 1502, Louis XII d'Orléans was one of the invited guests.

The original layout was expanded and redecorated around 1560, when the residence took on ries, framed within pale stucco frames and beautiful frescoed herms.

The renovation of the building and the garden, laid out on the site of former vineyards and fruit orchards, has been attributed to the painter and architect Giovan Battista Castello, known as Il Bergamasco. This hypothesis is borne out by stylistic affinities seen throughout the composition and also in the garden, where a lovely nymphaeum supports the stairs leading to the

The Rape of the Sabines, by Luca Cambiaso, in the Villa Imperiale, Terralba (Genoa).

Opposite: Principal facade of the Villa Cambiaso, Genoa.

an appearance very similar to its current state. On that occasion the building's most characteristic elements—cornices, stringcourses, corbels, tympanums, and loggias—were added. Two side loggias are supported by columns with fanciful capitals resting on balustrades. The entrance, off-center on the left, leads to a foyer that in turn leads to the celebrated drawing room where the Genovese painter Luca Cambiaso frescoed his *Rape of the Sabines* (1560–1570), one of his best works. The composition, given depth by artificial perspectives, is surrounded by refined lesser sto-

terraces that that holds the villa. The original green space was transformed in 1875 according to the prevailing Romantic taste, with cypresses, cedars, and other exotic plants introduced to an area that already had "avenues crowded with rosebushes." A few years later, in 1909, then-owner Cesare Imperiale, added a nymphaeum at the back of the villa; inspired by sixteenth-century tastes, it harmonized the facade facing the hillside with the other terraces.

The Villa Cambiaso stood isolated at the center of a garden, commissioned by a member of the

nobility, Luca Giustiniani, who entrusted the design to Galeazzo Alessi. Completed in 1548, the villa immediately inspired many other projects, thanks to its distinctive character, mediated by Alessi's Roman influences. The compact block, the tripartite composition of the facade, and the plastic decorative scheme with orders, tympanums, and balustrades, echoed analogous solutions adopted earlier by Antonio da Sangallo the Younger.

Two loggias, on the east and west sides, intercede between the closed and open space, passing through the generating core of the design, made up of the atrium–staircase–drawing room. The latter was frescoed at the beginning of the century by Antonio Quinzio, though his *Naval Victory* was unfortunately lost during a bombardment in 1944. The piano nobile represents the culminating feature of the composition, with its rich architectural details and geometric, botanical, and anthropomorphic motifs, in an ensemble that is at times Raphaelesque. Only the principal facade is embellished by architectural orders, creating a privileged entrance axis resembling a theatrical set.

In the Villa Cambiaso, perhaps for the first time, the villa was freed from ties to agricultural property. There was property, but it was designed for diversion and repose, amid beautiful gardens that explicated a purely ornamental and recreational function. In 1787 the residence was brought by Caterina Pellegrina Giustiniani as part of her dowry in her marriage to a Cambiaso, whose family retained ownership until 1921.

Beginning in the sixteenth century, the Riviera to the west of the city, once rich in fertile lands, became a pleasant setting for aristocratic dwellings for the city's intelligentsia. Gradually luxuriant Italian-style gardens and dense, romantic parks replaced farmland, reinventing the local flora.

The Villa Doria Pamphili was built just outside the fourteenth-century walls, near the Porta di San Tommasso. This villa-fortress was commissioned by Andrea Doria, one of the leading figures in early-sixteenth-century Genoa. The prince had achieved success as a prison contractor for Emperor Charles V, and he had spent time

at the major Renaissance courts. For this reason his unbridled ambition, and particularly themes related to his ascent to power, became the subject matter of the decorative cycle of the villa.

The complex was formed from the merging of three properties acquired beginning in 1521. Construction took place in successive phases, and by 1533, when Emperor Charles V stayed there, the work already had reached a satisfactory stage. Its size is notable, stretching from the sea almost up to the summit of the Granarolo hill. The area

Above: The turn-of-the-century Villa Gaslini in Genoa; top, a bust from the garden of the Villa Doria Pamphili in Genoa.

Opposite: The garden of the Villa Doria Pamphili.

is subdivided into terraces, with various gardens to the sides. The main building, designed as the owner's residence, is flanked by two side wings that housed service areas (oven, kitchens, quarters for servants and guards, granaries, and stables), which guaranteed a certain self-sufficiency for the complex, which also had its own landing area.

Above: The nymphaeum of the Villa Imperiale Scassi, Genoa; right, the building's main facade.

The decorations of the rooms were carried out almost exclusively by a single artist, Pietro Buonaccorsi, known as Perin del Vaga. This work celebrated the grand destiny of the patron, identifying Doria with Neptune, god of the sea, flanked by Jupiter, god of the earth, and an evident allegory of Charles V. Even the facades were frescoed, with the south face bearing a representation of the history of Jason and the Golden Fleece. In 1671 Giannan-

A curious collage of inset majolica on the facade of the Villa Gaslini, Genoa.

drea III Doria married Anna Pamphili and moved to Rome; this marked the beginning of the villa's decline. There were moments of glory once again in the nineteenth century, when Napoleon (1803) and Victor Emmanuel (1815) stayed there.

The noble Villa Imperiale Scassi was built around 1560 for Vincenzo Imperiale, one of the most visible members of Genoa's mercantile aristocracy. It was erected in the center of Samper-darena, an area where numerous other villas were being built. The structure is slightly set back from the street, and the hill that rises behind it contains a park, originally larger than it is now; dominated by a magnificent view, this park included a fish-pond, parterres, and a nymphaeum placed on axis with the villa. Today the fountain of Neptune and another, smaller nymphaeum with a figure of Atlas remain. The typology and style recall that of

Galeazzo Alessi. The imposing facade is made up of Doric half columns and Corinthian pilaster strips alternating in a decidedly Mannerist style. The original plaster had a faux-marble finish, red on the back wall and pink in the relief elements.

The interior decorations are from the early seventeenth century and were commissioned by Gian Vincenzo Imperiale, known in the city for his work as commissioner of construction for the new city walls. The atrium of the house is dominated by elegant grotesques that frame a fresco depicting Samson felling the wild beast, which might refer to an event in the patron's life. The second floor depicts

stands on the site of a castle built in 1320 by Anfreone Spinola, a Ghibelline. Traces of this structure remained when, in the second half of the seventeenth century, work began on the villa. Although the first mention of this villa dates back only to 1712, it is clear that the layout is

Above: Villa Duchessa di Galliera in Genoa.

Right: The turn-of-the-century Villino Luxoro, in Nervi (Genoa).

other mythological themes; some rooms have rococo stucco decorations, introduced during an eighteenth-century restoration. Neoclassical elements were added during work undertaken in 1801, when the complex was acquired by Onofrio Scassi, an illustrious doctor and scholar.

The present day Villa Duchessa di Galliera

from the seventeenth century, and additions were then made in 1780.

The complex rises between the Leira River and the beach upriver from the town of Voltri. It is reached via a tree-lined avenue, which terminates in a broad open space from which two flights of stairs rise to a terrace, upon which the villa stands. The staircase seems off-center from the perspectival axis of the construction because it leads to the main entrance, along a side facade.

The main house, flanked by low buildings of a more recent date and surmounted by the coat of arms of the Brignole family, has an impressive puppet theater, decorated in trompe-l'oeil by Canepa, with a lantern on the ceiling that allowed it to be used in the daytime. In 1788 an oratory was built within the villa. But the villa reached its greatest splendor in the nineteenth century, when the complex still was called the Villa Brignole

appearance, although in fact it is not as large as it seems. The ground floor corresponds almost exclusively to a containing wall for the basement level of the villa. Along the back a small courtyard encloses a charming winter garden, with a nymphaeum with statues of Bacchus and David.

The interior contains a graceful neoclassical Sale, after the family that owned it. The most famous member of this family, Maria, duchess of Galliera, not only renamed the villa but also carried out a considerable expansion and embellishments. Illustrious guests were numerous, from Pope Pius VII, to Ferdinando VII, king of Naples, to Wilhelm II of Germany.

The neoclassical facade of the Villa Grüber, Genoa. The facade opens onto a large park.

LOMBARDY

BETWEEN THE LAKES AND THE PO

The first fifteenth-century Lombard villas were built for the most part in the vicinity of large towns, as rural dwellings for the Renaissance courts, for whom these buildings symbolized their conquest of the region. The Villa Ghirardina in Motteggiana, near Mantua, is a case in point, erected by the Gonzaga family along the

reached until the eighteenth century, later than other regions such as Tuscany, the Veneto, or Latium. Lombardy was no longer playing a primary role in Italian architecture, for numerous and varied reasons. The plague of 1630 had depopulated city and countryside, and the consequent economic recession was aggravated by the repeated

banks of the Po so they could control navigation there. It is important to remember that waterways—rivers, canals, shipping lanes, lakes—offered the most rapid and secure means of travel until the advent of the railroad, and even then rail routes long remained scarce.

Although there were numerous and refined examples from the sixteenth and seventeenth centuries, the high point for Lombard villas was not

passage of foreign armies. Moreover, echoes of Counter-Reformation severity found a dutiful interpreter in Cardinal Carlo Borromeo, and his commanding advocation of austerity (although broadly intended) surely dampened building ambitions. Only in the provinces of Cremona and Mantua—geographically and traditionally more independent from Milan than other regions—did private building activity continue, with important

One of the numerous villas that overlook Lake Como.

Opposite: Villa Mina della Scala, Casteldidone (Cremona); the villa's fortified appearance is softened by the garden that surrounds it.

creations, such as the Villa Mina della Scala in Casteldidone, or La Favorita in Porto Mantovano.

In the region of Cremona, villas were built in the plain between the Oglio and Po Rivers, while in the area of Crema they were concentrated in the plain between the Serio and Adda Rivers. In Mantua, in addition to being built along the Po and the Mincio, villas also were scattered in the direction of Lake Garda. The provinces of Sondrio and Pavia, despite being located at opposite ends of the region, with rather different terrains, share an almost total absence of villas, although Pavia has an abundance of castles. The frivolous migrations

of patrons in search of better climates and views contrasted with the more pragmatic and deliberate movements of artists. As early as the fifteenth century the Florentine Luca Fancelli, designer of the Villa Ghirardina and other villas in the area of Mantua, was active at the Gonzaga court. Like him, many others were engaged by the humanist courts to contribute to a new artistic flowering. Mantua was particularly receptive in this regard. In the sixteenth century Giulio Romano worked there, having moved away from Rome and the school of Raphael. Giuseppe Dattari, author of the Castello di Bosco della Fontana in Marmirolo, also was active, as was Nicolò Sebregondi, who designed La Favorita, the phantasmagoric suburban residence of the Gonzaga family.

The Castello di Bosco Fontana, ancient hunting lodge of the Gonzaga family in Marmirolo (Mantua); near left, the elevation of the principal facade.

GIULIO ROMANO

ROME, 1499–MANTUA, 1546

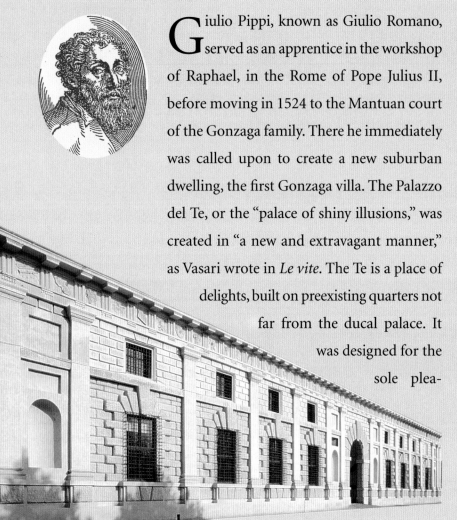

Palazzo del Te, Mantua; a side entrance (above) and the series of courtyards (opposite).

Giulio Pippi, known as Giulio Romano, served as an apprentice in the workshop of Raphael, in the Rome of Pope Julius II, before moving in 1524 to the Mantuan court of the Gonzaga family. There he immediately was called upon to create a new suburban dwelling, the first Gonzaga villa. The Palazzo del Te, or the "palace of shiny illusions," was created in "a new and extravagant manner," as Vasari wrote in *Le vite*. The Te is a place of delights, built on preexisting quarters not far from the ducal palace. It was designed for the sole pleasure of Duke Federico II Gonzaga, who would dine there for lunch or dinner. The villa represents the highlight of a period of intense meditation on Renaissance stylistic elements, and it would become a point of reference, first for early Mannerist projects, then for clearly Baroque work, for patrons and designers throughout the region. The duke was explicit in his inscribed dedication of the villa to his mistress, noblewoman Isabella Boschetti: "Quod huic deest me tor-quet" or "what she lacks torments me."

Gonzaga's passion inspired the decoration of the new dwelling. The celebration of nature, the influence of the stars, and mythological narrative are the themes Giulio Romano undertook for the private rapture of Gonzaga and his lover in frescoes located in the private apartments, a delicious counterpoint to the stiff official nature of the ducal palace. But the culmination of the decorative scheme is seen in the representation of the wedding banquet of Cupid and Psyche, permeated by an exquisite licentiousness that must refer to personal events in the life of Federico, sublimated into the learned mythological quotation.

A passage through the rooms leaves the viewer amazed by the effectiveness of the extreme foreshortening, what Vasari called the *sotto in sù* view. The gaze upward traverses the ethereal vaults to break through into an illusory and endless world. Having learned the "grand manner" from the master, Raphael, Giulio Romano celebrated a world of appearances, where the most recondite dreams could become reality. As the physical space is decontextualized, the perspectival play becomes an end in itself, giving life to one of the most suggestive examples of an *ante litteram* surrealism.

COMO AND VARESE

"**N**othing in the world can compare to the charm of these scorching summer days, passed on the lakes around Milan amid chestnut groves, so green you think they have dipped their branches in the water." Thus Stendhal (1783–1842) described his moments of relaxation along Lake Como, in his *Italian Journey* (1817). "Milanese who feel the cold spend the winter there; the palaces multiply on the green of the hillsides and are mirrored in the waters. It is too much to say palaces, and not enough to call them country houses."

He credited the special charm of the lake area, whose villages of Tremezzo, Bellagio, and Varenna enchanted patrons at first sight, for the notable prestige of dwellings along the Lario. On Lake Maggiore, villas were built for the most part along the Piedmont shore, concentrated between Stresa and Verbania, while this sort of dwelling was clearly less prevalent around Lake Garda, where castles abounded.

In Varese, rural dwellings were scattered in the amphitheater of hills that ringed the city. While lakeside or mountain views were valued, the buildings were sited off to the side, rejecting the idea of the grand facade or the theatrical backdrop.

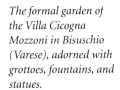

The formal garden of the Villa Cicogna Mozzoni in Bisuschio (Varese), adorned with grottoes, fountains, and statues.

BRIANZA

Builders of villas particularly coveted the area of Brianza, characterized by rolling hills, where the climate was good and agriculture had flourished for centuries. Villas as feudal symbols, austere emblems of territorial possession, were gradually joined by frivolous holiday dwellings. Places such as Montesoro, Arcore, Meda and Besana became the new social centers in the Brianza region.

The people of Milan built their first holiday houses around Brianza or along the banks of the canals. Not until the turn of the nineteenth century, when new means of communication arose, did the urban aristocracy move out toward the

for the urban patrician class, on their large estates. These were seasonal dwellings, often the result of the transformation of modest preexisting, sometimes fortresslike structures, replacing the enclosed garden or orchard with a garden designed for the owner's pleasure and recreation during respites from work.

The proliferation of vacation dwellings in the eighteenth century was stimulated by the emergence of medium-sized properties, carved out from the gradual division of the grand medieval estates. Moreover, the first period of Austrian rule (1710–1740) brought an increase in the

Below: The Villa Cazzola in Arcore (Milan) dates back to the second half of the sixteenth century.

Left: An elevation of the facade by Carlo Amati, built in 1812 during the last renovation.

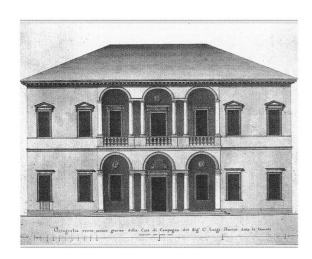

lakes. First veritable palaces arose along the canals. These were inward-looking structures, organized around a courtyard; only in the eighteenth century were villas built with an orientation to large geometric gardens, with terraces and wharves. Important residences also were built far from the water, such as the Vertemate Franchi palace in Piuro, the Villa Cicogna Mozzoni in Bisuschio, or the Villa Litta Invernizzi in Trenzanesio. But most of the villas were built

GIAN BATTISTA SOMMARIVA

LODI, 1760–MILAN, 1826

The Villa Clerici (today the Villa Carlotta) in Tremezzo, on Lake Como, was commissioned by the family of the same name, toward the end of the seventeenth century. In 1801 it was sold to Gian Battista Sommariva, then president of the governing committee of the Cisalpine Republic. At the time he purchased the villa, Sommariva headed the government of Milan and needed

Garden (above) and facade (opposite) of the Villa Carlotta in Tremezzo (Como). The villa was built in 1690 at the edge of the lake, for Giorgio Clerici.

a dwelling to celebrate his new status. Having begun as an obscure lawyer from the provinces, he succeeded in rapidly building his career, thanks in part to questionable favors he granted to the Napoleonic armies.

Sommariva's power was not long-lived, however; in 1802 his influence declined, and not even his influential friendships could recover his lost status. Despite the brevity of his glory, he accumulated tremendous assets and became one of the wealthiest men in Europe. He moved to Paris, into a large palace on the rue Basse des Remparts, where he became famous for his activities as a

patron and collector; Antonio Canova was one of the artists who enjoyed his favor. His incredible and heterogeneous collection was crammed into his palaces in Paris and Tremezzo. Although the latter was his vacation home, it was there he held grand festivities and receptions, competing with the Melzi d'Eril family, who were filling their own dwelling on the opposite lakeshore with a more modest collection of works.

While Sommariva nurtured a sincere passion for art, particularly sculpture, his reputation as a patron also helped obscure his less than exemplary past. Moreover he did not forget that art was always a good investment. His villa in Tremezzo was perfect for these public relations activities, attracting visitors from throughout Europe. Inside the villa, Gian Battista installed rooms draped with silks, mirrors, and lamps to set off the works in his collection, which he also had reproduced in engravings, lacquers, miniatures, and other small objects of everyday use.

Upon Sommariva's death in 1826, the villa and the palace in Paris were found to be filled with works of art, some of great value, others of dubious attribution and taste. Fortunately the villa was sold "as is," with its collection intact, and since then few works have been sold.

presence of the nobility—which included military figures, officials, and financiers, rewarded for their loyalty to the empire—creating a class of new potential patrons socially positioned between the feudal nobility and the bourgeoisie. An economic revival resulted in the heyday of the Lombard villas, between the arrival of the Austrians and the first two decades of the nineteenth century. While this period was not very long, much was achieved in architecture.

MILAN

It is fortunate that the high point for villas in Lombardy occurred between the eighteenth and nineteenth centuries, precisely when the greatest artistic personalities were at work. Giovanni Ruggeri, who studied in Rome under Carlo Fontana and Gian Lorenzo Bernini, was one of the most prolific architects, building the Villa Arconati in Bollate, the Villa Alari Visconti in Cernusco sul Naviglio, and the Villa Cavazzi della Somaglia in Orio Litta, as well as the impressive Castello Visconti Citterio in Brignano Gera d'Adda, clearly his greatest work. Francesco Croce was another representative of the late Baroque period in Lom-

Below: The courtyard of the Villa Alari Visconti in Cernusco sul Naviglio (Milan).

Right: Engraving by Marc'Antonio Dal Re, depicting the same villa, then known as the Villa Alari.

Opposite: The ruins of the Villa Archinto in Robecco sul Naviglio (Milan).

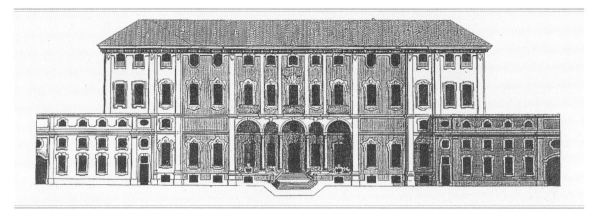

bardy, midway between rococo and neoclassicism. Well known in Milan, he presided over the building of the Duomo from 1732 to 1773 and also designed the Villa Brentano in Corbetta. Simone Cantone (or Cantoni), an architect from Ticino with many projects in Genoa and Milan, worked in a more strictly neoclassical vein. His language is severe and monumental, as seen in the Villa Giovio and the Villa Olmo in Como, built toward the end of the eighteenth century.

With the birth of the Cisalpine Republic, artists such as Giuseppe Piermarini and Leopold Pollack,

GIUSEPPE PIERMARINI

FOLIGNO, 1734–MILAN, 1808

Giuseppe Piermarini, the prophet of neo-classicism in Lombardy, was a disciple of Gaspare Vanvitelli. He worked with the master on the Villa Reale at Caserta before moving to Milan. In 1776 he began teaching at the Brera, and three years later he was named imperial royal architect. His projects include the Villa Cusani di Desio (at least the principal facade), the royal palace in Monza, and the Villa Borromeo d'Adda in Cassano d'Adda. In addition to palaces and villas, he also involved himself in urban planning. His work served as a point of reference for neo-classical architecture in Lombardy during the second half of the eighteenth century, shaping an entire generation of architects. The Viennese architect Leopold Pollack was one of the most significant artistic personalities in Piermarini's circle. First a student, then the master's assistant, Pollack became one of

the favorite architects of the Milanese nobility. In addition to the Villa Belgioioso, later the royal palace in Milan, he designed the Villa Amalia in Erba, the Villa Antona Traversi in Meda, and the Villa Pesenti in Paladina, where he also oversaw the layout of the Romantic park. Pollack's language was classical, courtly, and in some ways neo-Palladian; his vocabulary was clearly quite similar to that of Piermarini, in the way it fully satisfied the patron's desire for stateliness. This language also confirms the extent to which much Milanese architecture from the second half of the eighteenth century inspired and guided the neoclassical style in Lombardy. Today, the greatest example of this contribution can be seen in the Villa Borromeo d'Adda, designed by Piermarini in the 1780s as a transformation of a preexisting Baroque structure. This intervention in the landscape influenced architectural development throughout Cassano, giving the town an indelible appearance.

The imposing principal facade of the eighteenth-century Villa Borromeo d'Adda in Cassano d'Adda (Milan).

Villa Visconti Maineri in Cassinetta di Lugagnano (Milan), the facade facing the canal. The surrounding wall encloses the garden.

who had made their names working for the Austrians, soon were shunted aside in favor of their disciples and new figures. These included architect Luigi Cagnola, an aristocrat by birth who, after studying in Rome, launched the Napoleonic transformation of Milan. His Villa Rotonda in Inverigo is imbued with an unconditional admiration for Hellenic and Roman architecture. The Ticinese architect Giocondo Albertolli was a student of Piermarini, and they worked together on the Villa

Scala and on the Villa Reale in Monza. Albertolli also designed the Villa Melzi d'Eril in Bellagio.

Noteworthy garden designer Luigi Canonica, assisted by agronomist Luigi Villoresi, was responsible for one of the most impressive landscape settings in Italy, the park of the Villa Reale in Monza. Both its extensive scope and its Romantic style—already in vogue in Great Britain, but not yet firmly rooted in Italy and Lombardy—would have a lasting influence on Italian landscape designers.

BERGAMO AND BRESCIA

In Bergamo and Brescia, villas were built rather close to the main cities. On the other hand these two cities are located between the plain and the Alpine foothills, in a setting known for its pleasant climate and views. Here villas were for the most part connected to large and profitable farms. The small town of Stezzano, for example, became famous for silkworm production as well for its four aristocratic dwellings. Most rural res-

Left: The courtyard of the eighteenth-century Castello Visconti Citterio in Brignano Gera d'Adda (Bergamo), by architect Giovanni Ruggeri.

Below: The Villa Zanchi Antona Traversi, in Mapello (Bergamo), built between the seventeenth and eighteenth centuries.

idences were inhabited only intermittently, since nearby Brescia had a considerable number of urban palaces, perhaps more than any other city in Lombardy.

A recurring typology in this region is characterized by a U-shaped plan with an internal courtyard at the center. This courtyard, which undoubtedly had its origins in the castle, was abandoned in other regions as early as the sixteenth century but survived here until the eighteenth. The expression of a clear tendency toward introversion, in contrast to the more

Above: The neoclassical tympanum of the Villa Mazzucchelli in Mazzano (Brescia).

Right: The nymphaeum of the Villa Bettoni, Bogliaco in Gargnano (Brescia), on Lake Garda. The structure was built behind the villa and is separated from it by a public road.

open villas of the Veneto or Tuscany, the internal courtyard reveals an unstable, tentative relationship with the surrounding landscape. It represents a desire to focus—within a single, well-defined space—functions tied to the lives of both the proprietors and the service personnel.

In these early, austere, closed complexes, spatial continuity did not move beyond the interior courtyard–drawing room–garden axis, and only with the second-story loggias did the building open onto the landscape. But beginning in the sixteenth century, projects such as the Villa Lechi in Erbusco began to be introduced into the

region. Its porticoed wings are joined with seamless grace and elegance to the main building, anticipating the U typology that later spread throughout Lombardy, up until the neoclassical period. Other recurring elements are the portico around the courtyard and the two drawing rooms. The ground-floor drawing room was used as a foyer during balls; the drawing room on the second floor was reached by a grand staircase that led up from the portico. The piano nobile drawing room, used as a ballroom, was generally richly decorated and had a balcony for musicians, for life in these villas often was enlivened by, banquets, balls, and evenings of music.

These villas also were characterized by one or more axes of symmetry, which suggested an itinerary for the visitor, a sort of ideal taking in of all the spaces of the house and garden. These axes sometimes intersected, but without generating dynamic effects on the space. In fact additional viewpoints were never sought, and the panoramic views continued to be valued as such, for themselves, giving the composition a certain static quality. Some critics have seen this peculiarity of Lombard villas—unable to completely break away from late Mannerist influences, even when the phantasmagoric Baroque compositions spreading through Italy suggested a more

dynamic use of space—as a limitation.

Nonetheless, eighteenth-century villas, despite their axes and rigid geometry, had a stronger relationship to the surrounding environment than their Romantic counterparts. The latter, while not taking advantage of artificially delimited spaces, became increasingly isolated at the center of a park. Although there were no physical barriers, they became less approachable than earlier projects, whose tall gates at least permitted visual access. At the same time enclosing walls were replaced by dense vegetation, which added a new formal value to the overall composition.

Above: The long perspectival axis of the Villa Fenaroli in Rezzato (Brescia) starts at the gate, passes through the villa, and ascends the hill beyond.

Left: The Villa Mazzucchelli in Mazzano (Brescia), built in the mid-eighteenth century at the behest of Count Giovan Maria Mazzucchelli, a man of letters.

MARC'ANTONIO DAL RE
BOLOGNA, 1697–MILAN, 1766

Marc'Antonio Dal Re, a young artist from Bologna, moved to Milan after a stay in Cremona, where he learned the art of engraving. In the Lombard capital he opened a printing house and became an entrepreneur, publishing his own engravings and those of some of his collaborators. His enterprise, similar to Giorgio Vasari's in Rome or Richard Wagner's in Venice, was only intermittently successful, and upon his death he left some 9,000 lire in debts. His collection of engravings of the villas of Milan, *Ville di delizia o siano palagi camparecci nello Stato di Milano*, is without doubt his most famous work, although the collection of eighty-eight urban views of Milan is much more appreciated. *Ville di delizia* appeared in two separate editions, the first published in a single volume in 1726, the second in two tomes in 1743. The one-volume publication documents eight villas in various plates, while the two-volume work reprints three from the earlier publication and adds nine new ones. The subjects are illustrated with more engravings, which

Above: Villa Pertusani, view of the garden. Elegant figures animate the garden, delineated by box-tree topiaries.

Opposite: Villa in Corbetta, with its elaborately scrolled parterres.

often vary from one edition to the other. Thus in practical terms these can be treated as two different works. Dal Re planned to create a six-volume work, but published only three. He continued to make engravings, but without collecting the plates into a volume for publication, and it is likely that he was impeded by financial difficulties. Although the artist carefully tailored his representations of villas and gardens to satisfy his patrons' wishes, sales of his books still did not amount to enough to cover his expenses. This may explain why the quality of the engravings is much higher in the first edition, where the signature of Johannes Baptista Ricaldus appears as draftsman, a signature absent from the second edition. Evidently Dal Re tried to save money by doing the entire second edition on his own. In any case, he did document twenty-one villas in various plates, all republished in the edition reissued in 1973 by Il Polifilo, which also includes reproductions of some loose sheets now at the A. Bertarelli Civic Print Collection in Milan. During the first half of the eighteenth century, important works were built on a considerable scale, but also as the result of refined design; Dal Re captured this crucial moment in the evolution of the Milanese villa.

CREMONA

The territory of Cremona lies at the center of the Po Valley, delimited to the south by the Po River, in a particularly fertile region, rich in waterways. At first a Roman colony, the city in the Middle Ages was ruled by church bishops, before being established as a commune and entering in conflict with Milan. In 1334 Cremona surrendered to Azzone Visconti and remained under the rule of the dukedom until 1509.

Milan played a leading role in Lombardy, and the first villas arose in its environs; not until the second half of the sixteenth century were the first elegant rural residences in Cremona built. Unlike other cities such as Mantua, Ferrara, or Milan, Cremona was not a capital, and its stately dwellings reflect various influences brought by a succession of rulers, such as the Milanese or the Venetians. Nonetheless, numerous villas and castles dot the territory, bearing witness to a former opulence and the nobility's desire for a well-to-do life. The composition of these buildings is typical: main residence, garden and/or park embellished with greenhouses, small lakes, temples, towers, and aviaries. Some areas were strictly private and reserved for the secluded pleasure of the master and his guests, while others were public, frequented by peasants,

Right: The interior courtyard of the Castello Manfredi in Cicognolo (Cremona). Despite the building's appearance, it dates to the nineteenth century.

Opposite: The Villa Medici del Vascello in San Giovanni in Croce (Cremona). This eighteenth-century dwelling was built upon a fourteenth-century castle.

merchants, performers, wayfarers, and curiosity seekers.

The typology of these villas in many ways evolved from that of the castle, which gradually lost its defensive features, preserving its character as a building inserted within nature, a healthy alternative to city life, situated in a strategic position at the center of vast landholdings. Some dwellings arose on a pre-existing fortress, reutilizing its towers, crenellated walls, and foundations. Others continued the castle's enclosed courtyard, and still others had a U-shaped court, introducing new elements now that a defensive function was no longer necessary. The phenomenon took on different connotations in the nineteenth century, when the reinterpretive process was interrupted. A proliferation of faux stylistic quotations was typical of the Romantic revival of neo-castles, which spread rapidly throughout Cremona and its territory and even took hold in the region of Mantua, a neighboring area with a similar history.

Nevertheless ties to the land always remained clear. The Cremona nobility—unlike that in other areas—never rejected its rustic origins, and its residences, reflecting this agrarian bias, became centers of activity for their annexed landholdings. Curiously, their dwellings have for the most part preserved this role, to a degree not

Villa Strozzi in Begozzo (Mantua). The current layout dates to the eighteenth century but the original building is from the sixteenth century.

found elsewhere, to this day, giving them a charm that merits a journey of discovery.

The town of Crema always maintained an independent history, although in some ways it paralleled that of nearby Cremona. Its artistic activity, a direct emanation of the larger city's power, nevertheless had its own peculiar characteristics. Moreover, because of Crema's greater proximity to Milan and Bergamo, new ideas arrived there first. This mix of influences undoubtedly stimulated the distinctive development of villas in Crema. Far from being homogeneous, each has a story all its own. This originality is manifested in the rejection of the castle typology favored by designers from Mantua and Cremona, who on numerous occasions insisted until the late nineteenth century on reproposing frivolous crenellated little castles.

In Crema these forms are unusual, although some dwellings were built upon fortified structures. It is clear that there was not one single, continuous period of artistic activity here, but rather a succession of episodes, each with its own characteristics and style. Careful examination shows a heterogeneity that is the result of a vigorous and intolerant spirit, but one that clearly was also cultivated and majestic. The decadent charm of these aristocratic dwellings is enchanting, and in any case they merit a visit, to get beyond their romantic allure and understand their strict relationship with the surrounding landscape.

MANTUA

After Urbino and Ferrara, Mantua was the last capital of the late fifteenth century. The territory was conquered by the Gonzaga family in 1328, displacing the Bonacolsi family, until then the powerful masters of the city. From that time on the ascent of the Gonzaga family was inexorable, and their enlightened rule converted the small town into one of the most vibrant humanist courts.

The succession of artists kept pace with changes in political and cultural moods: from Pisanello to Andrea Mantegna, from Raphael to Vittore Carpaccio, to Antonio Allegri Correggio, from Leon Battista Alberti to Luca Fancelli, to Luciano Laurana and then to Giulio Romano. There were always many artists at work, constantly engaged and were emulated by members of the enterprising Mantuan court. Influential guests were received in these decentralized but sumptuous residences, entertained by comedians and clowns and sometimes pressed into interminable shooting parties with rare and prized dogs and horses.

At the height of the dukedom's success and fame, Federico II Gonzaga, who came to power in 1519 after a youth spent amid the splendors of papal Rome, invited Giulio Romano, a student of Raphael, to Mantua. He was entrusted with the construction of the Palazzo del Te, which would become the residence of Federico's lover, the noblewoman Isabella Boschetti.

The powerful Mannerist reverberations of Giulio Romano's creations acted as a backdrop to

Below left: Elevation of the facade of the Villa Strozzi in Begozzo.

Below: The ruins of La Favorita, in Porto Mantovano (Mantua), a seventeenth-century work by Nicolò Sebregondi.

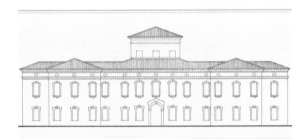

in feverish activity. Isabella d'Este, the young wife of the eclectic Francesco Gonzaga, fostered a sober and refined atmosphere that soon brought great prestige to the city. The humanist school of Vittorino da Feltre acted as a crucible for the new generation of Mantuan rulers.

The expansion of the dukedom entailed a careful commitment to the consolidation of the Gonzaga presence in the new territories. During this phase of conquest, the Gonzagas built fortifications and rural residences at key points within their territory. These proved to be fundamental,

the dukedom's progressive and inexorable decline. Guglielmo Gonzaga's ascension to power was a warning sign, and his successors—prodigal libertines known for their splendid banquets and endless festivities—brought to a head a crisis of ideals as well as finances, culminating in the construction of the costly suburban villa known as La Favorita. A small, *ante litteram* Versailles, La Favorita was built at the behest of Cardinal Ferdinando Gonzaga for his licentious court,

needs. With increasing frequency, palace and villa merged the functions of residence and servants' quarters, in order to fully utilize all available rooms. Property was broken up, and immense parcels of land, once ruled by nobles devoted principally to safeguarding their privileges, passed into the hands of a strongly motivated and entrepreneurial landed bourgeoisie. In this new world, the noble villas and palaces became decontextualized. The expense of main-

Right: The Villa l'Arrigona in San Giacomo delle Segnate (Mantua), the seventeenth-century dwelling of the Arrigoni family, who originally came from the Taleggio Valley.

Opposite: The Villa Vimercati Sanseverino in Vaiano Cremasco (Cremona), surrounded by a delicate boxwood broderie.

which soon abandoned it, allowing it to fall into ruin.

At this point the cultural atmosphere was a far cry from the learned iconography Andrea Mantegna had depicted in the Camera Picta of the ducal palace. Even as the great art collections were being sold to England, the last Gonzagas, unable to believe in the waning of a myth, squandered what little remained on their sumptuous town residence. In the provinces, their villas and palaces were sold off to the nascent landed bourgeoisie, which adapted them to its own tastes and

taining them could not be justified by the pragmatic new entrepreneurial class, which in turn abandoned them.

The fate of these residences, once opulent, lively, and representative, was varied. Some were destroyed, and many others were transformed into warehouses and sometimes abandoned. A few have been preserved as courtly dwellings. Like the Palladian villas in the Veneto or those in Medici Tuscany, after the insults of abandonment, these in recent times have once more found new roles, suitable to their nobility.

THE NORTHEAST

VENETO

EMILIA-ROMAGNA

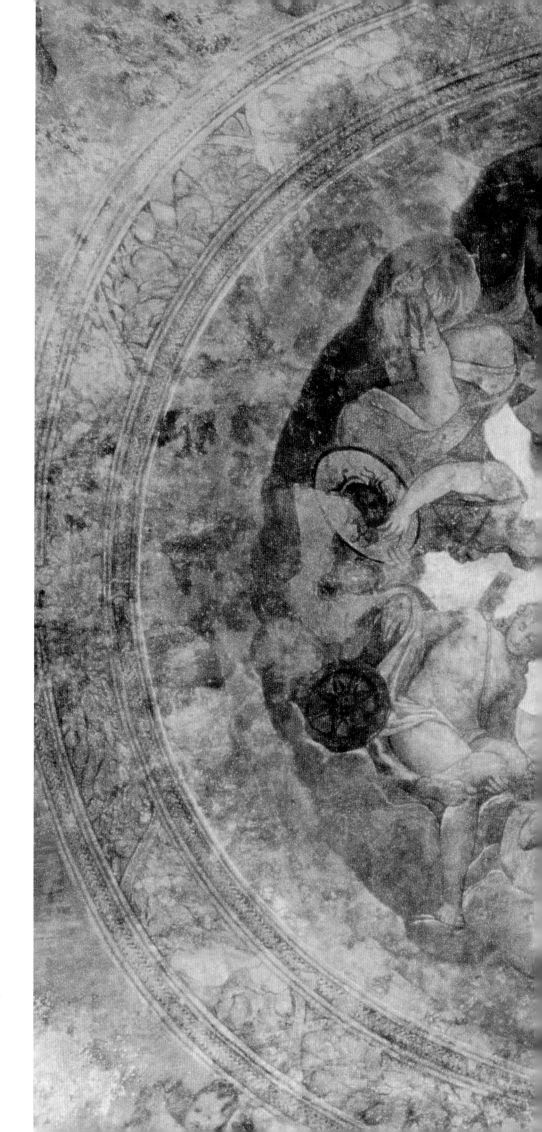

VENETO

Venetian Echoes

The sublime inland residences where the Venetian nobility spent their holidays were wonderfully integrated into the surroundings, becoming active and inevitable components of the landscape. Piers, gardens, statues, and other signs along the Brenta Riviera or on the banks of numerous canals announced the presence of these elegant dwellings.

But not everyone looked kindly upon this fashion for country villas. Niccolò Machiavelli in particular spoke rather harshly about it in his *Discourses*, referring to the Venetian nouveaux riches in the withering tones of the old aristocracy: "Gentlemen in that Republic are so more in name than in fact; for they have no great revenues from estates, their riches being founded upon

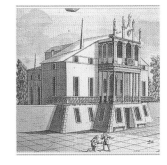

Left: Villa Pisani in Stra, on the Brenta Riviera; an engraving (above) depicting the villa in the seventeenth century.

Pages 88–89: Ceiling fresco from the drawing room of the Villa Caldogno, built in the Caldogno region in the mid-sixteenth century (Vicenza).

commerce and movable property, and moreover none of them have castles or jurisdiction over subjects, but the name of gentleman is only a title of dignity and respect, and is in no way based upon the things that gentlemen enjoy in other cities." The Venetian playwright Carlo Goldoni, in his preface to *Le smanie della villeggiature*, also complains that the vacationers have "poisoned the pleasures of the peasants and the shepherds."

The economic downturn of the eighteenth century was coming home to roost. A misguided

system of land use caused a slow but constant drop in production, which, coupled with the loss of a monopoly on trade, triggered an economic depression. Nevertheless, the well-to-do class, deaf to appeals for frugality, squandered its resources on increasingly dazzling rural residences, theaters for sumptuous festivities where they might ignore their now inexorable decline.

Villa Priuli in Oriago (Venice), as it currently appears (left), and in an engraving made after the seventeenth-century renovations (above).

PAOLO VERONESE

Paolo Calieri, known as Veronese, along with Titian and Tintoretto, is the third important figure in sixteenth-century Venetian painting. He studied in Verona at the school of Antonio Badile, before moving to Venice in 1553.

He is known for his sky-filled paintings, usually executed in fresco on the walls of both public and private palaces. He also painted, particularly in his early years, altarpieces and paintings on canvas. His themes and clowns in a representation of the life of Christ. As the scene moreover was presented as a cheerful gathering, losing any connotation of drama, Veronese was forced to change the name of the work to *Feast in the House of Levi.*

Of Veronese's works for villas, the series that brought him certain fame is in the Villa Barbaro in Maser, in the province of Treviso. Inserted into into Palladio's architecture, the artist's painting interweaves faux architec-

Courtesans looking out from a faux balcony in the Villa Barbaro, Maser (Treviso).

are both sacred and profane, befitting an artist at the height of his powers. His *Last Supper*, one of his masterpieces, gave him serious problems with the Inquisition, which felt it was blasphemous to include dwarves ture with figures that animate the composition, moving about in illusionistic worlds, enlivening and dematerializing the walls of the rooms. The life-size scale of these figures serves to amplify the illusory effect, and real-

ity and fiction become confused in the eye of the observer.

Veronese was particularly skilled in his use of perspective, which he would go on to demonstrate in other important works, not least his fresco *The Triumph of Venice*, in the Grand Council Hall of the ducal palace in Venice. Here the personified city is placed amid clouds at the center of turreted architecture, all depicted in a bold foreshortened perspective.

The drawing room of the Villa Barbaro: illusionistic architecture with figures.

VERONA

Lake Garda, the largest lake in Italy, lies between Lombardy, the Veneto, and Trentino Alto Adige; it is renowned above all for its climate, mild enough for lemon and olive trees, and its charming landscape. Its status as a holiday destination dates back to Roman times, as seen in the so-called Grottoes of Catullus of Sirmione, the ruins of a large imperial settlement that seems to have been frequented by the Latin poet. Since that time, numerous elegant dwellings have sprung up on the lake's shores, and its mountains have long served as a theater for territorial disputes between rival Milanese noble families, particularly the Della Scala and Visconti.

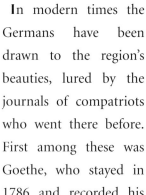
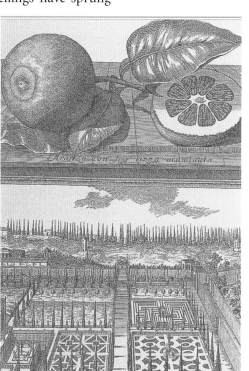

In modern times the Germans have been drawn to the region's beauties, lured by the journals of compatriots who went there before. First among these was Goethe, who stayed in 1786 and recorded his impressions in *Italian Journey*: "I could have been in Verona tonight (September 12), but I did not want to miss seeing Lake Garda and the magnificent natural scenery along its shores. . . . Here I am really in a new country, a totally unfamiliar environment. The people lead the careless life of a fool's paradise. To begin with, the doors have no locks, though the innkeeper assures me that I

Right: The celebrated garden of the Palazzo Giusti in Verona, in a 1714 engraving by Johann Cristoph Volkamer.

Opposite: The principal façade overlooking the garden of the Villa Allegri in Grezzano (Verona).

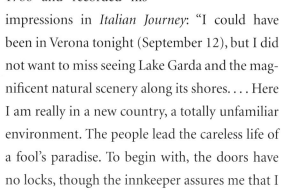

would not have to worry if all my belongings were made of diamonds. Then the windows are closed with oil paper instead of glass. . . . The women of the neighborhood chatter and shout all day long, but at the same time they all have something to do or attend to. I have yet to see one idle woman."

The following day Goethe took an adventurous boat ride: "At three o'clock this morning I set off with two rowers. At first the wind was favorable and they could use the sails. At dawn the wind dropped and the morning, though cloudy, was glorious. We passed Limone, whose terraced hillside gardens were planted with lemon trees, which made them look at once neat and lush. Each garden consists of rows of square white pillars, set some distance apart and mounting the hill in steps. Stout poles are laid across these pillars to give protection during the winter to the trees which have been planted between them. Our slow passage favored contemplation and observation of such pleasing details. We had already passed Malcesine when the wind suddenly veered right round and blew northwards, as it usually does during the day. Against its superior force, rowing was of no avail

Villa Bertoldi in Negrar (Verona), one of the first villas in the Veneto, dates to the late fifteenth century.

and we were compelled to land at the harbour of Malcesine, the first Venetian town on the eastern shore of the lake. When one has water to deal with, it is no good saying: 'Today I shall be in this place or that.' I shall make as good use of this stop as possible, in particular by drawing the castle, which is a beautiful building near the shore." Traveling along the Lake Garda road, the winding path that follows the banks, it is still possible to make a charming excursion among the most

refined residences of the region. These were sublime oases of peace, as well as elegant and eclectic status symbols, temporary quarters for a noble clientele that loved outdoor games, hunting, and boating, and maintained a principal residence elsewhere, in the major inland towns of the Veneto and Lombardy.

VICENZA

One of the first villas in the Veneto is the Villa da Porto in Thiene (Vicenza). Built during the second half of the fifteenth century on some pre-existing buildings, it is a good example of the transitional period between the castle-type dwelling and the actual villa. Its enclosing boundary, articulated by some structures and a tall, crenellated wall, delimits a large courtyard onto which the principal buildings open. The most significant of these is the owner's residence; here the facade is framed by two towers crowned by Ghibelline battlements with a purely decorative function. An airy portico on the ground floor and an elegant window subdivided into five Gothic arches, which evoke images of the Grand Canal in Venice, lighten the central portion of the building. Tall chimneys confirm the designer's Venetian inspiration. The interior boasts a painting cycle by Giovan Battista Zelotti; according to Vasari, there was another by Zelotti's master, Paolo Veronese, unfortunately now lost. The outbuildings include the famous stables designed by Francesco Muttoni and a Gothic oratory that dates to 1476.

The Villa Godi in Lonedo di Lugo is one of Palladio's earliest villa designs. It predates his sojourn in Rome, where he was exposed to the classical antiquities of that city, and his elaboration of the extremely personal vocabulary that would characterize his later production. This project, instead, clearly shows the influence of the more traditional style of Michele Sanmicheli, who was working in Venice during that period. Instead of a pronaos, typical of Palladio's mature work, the villa facade has an entrance wedged between two imposing wings, which look like two

Above: Villa da Porto in Thiene (Vicenza), built in the second half of the fifteenth century, on a preexisting structure.

Left: Villa Godi in Lonedo di Lugo (Vicenza), one of the first villas designed by Palladio.

towers. In its entirety, the composition, created between 1540 and 1542, is balanced, although the closed and severe design relates very little to the particularly lovely surrounding landscape. In his *Four Books on Architecture*, Palladio had earlier written, "The following building of Mr. Gerolamo di' Godi is in Lonedo and Vicentino, situated atop a hill with an extremely beautiful view, and next to a river that is used for fishing."

On the interior, frescoes by Zelotti and other Venetian artists depict battles and mythological episodes, alternating with trompe-l'oeil. The Hall of the Muses is particularly interesting; caryatids frame the south walls, dividing them into panels showing poets and muses inserted into archaic landscapes. Palladio commented that his patrons,

the noble Godi family, "didn't care about expenses" if it meant having the participation of the "most singular and excellent painters."

Around 1541, when Palladio received a commission to build a villa for the counts Vittore, Daniele, and Marco Pisani, who had vast landholdings in Lonigo, he came up with a design that can be interpreted in two ways. The facade overlooking the Guà River, which was still navigable, also faced the town of Lonigo, ruled by the Pisani family. Thus the building was meant to symbolize the patrons' power. But the facade that faced the lands behind the house was more open and serene, emphasizing the private and refined life, tied to the land and its production. Originally a castle stood on the site, and perhaps this

also served as a source of inspiration to Palladio.

This is one of the very first villas by Palladio that is documented with certainty. Important influences are evident, namely Giulio Romano's work in Mantua, particularly the Palazzo del Te. This is clearest in the facade overlooking the river, where, between two towers, three arcades open up, framed by rusticated Doric pilaster strips that support the tympanum, at the center of which is the patrons' coat of arms.

Regarding his most well known villa, La Rotonda, Palladio wrote, again in his *Four Books on Architecture*, that the site was "one of the most pleasant and delightful that can be found. . . . It is surrounded by sweet hills that offer the view of a

Above: Villa Pisani in Lonigo (Vicenza).

Left: The central hall of the Villa Caldogno in Caldogno (Vicenza). The sixteenth-century frescoes, which depict scenes of life in the villa, in faux architectural settings, are by Gianantonio Fasolo.

large amphitheater . . . and since there is a most beautiful view from all four sides, loggias were built on all the facades."

Paolo Almerico was a prelate from Vicenza, and after spending a long period at the papal court, he decided to pass his final years in the Veneto. He commissioned Palladio to build him a villa, which immediately become known as the "Ridond," or "La Rotonda." Dating remains uncertain, although recent studies suggest that work began around 1570. After the designer's death, construction was completed by Vincenzo Scamozzi, an architect from Vicenza who introduced significant changes, such as the lowering of the dome. This had been hemispherical in the original design, giving greater balance to the composition.

This sense of balance is key to understanding the entire complex, made up of a dado with four Ionic porticoes, each accessed by a flight of steps. A strict symmetry dominates the entire plan and focuses attention on the pivotal element of the composition. The eye of the dome represents an artificial extension of the top of the hillside on which the villa rests. Since the villa has a Greek-cross plan, it evokes the image of a basilica. With this project, Palladio achieved a brilliant synthesis of the idea of centrality, theorized by Donato Bramante and Michelangelo but almost never realized.

The circular drawing room is decorated with stuccowork and frescoes, some contemporary with the building and some from the seventeenth and eighteenth centuries. These might confuse the

The Villa Valmarana "Ai Nani" (or "Villa of the Dwarves") in Vicenza. The complex is made up of the main house, a storehouse, and a large guesthouse.

visitor about the actual dimensions of the building, and they work against the effect that Palladio sought. However, the interior's semidarkness, which prevails over the light that enters through the four corridors, invites the visitor to exit and admire the panorama of the Berici hills, which surround the villa. A series of divergent rays drawn on the floor emphasizes this centrifugal force.

La Rotonda is absolutely the most famous and most imitated villa in the Veneto. Goethe's visit there on September 21, 1786, was described in *Italian Journey*: "Today I went to see a magnificent house called the *Rotonda*. . . . The varied impression that this massive structure arouses in the wayfarer's glance, together with all its projecting columns, is truly extraordinary. . . . And just as the

Maria Bertolo, a jurist from Vicenza and the owner of vast lands just outside the city, commissioned the villa, built around 1665. The guest quarters and stables date to the early eighteenth century, when the villa had already passed into the hands of the Valmarana family.

One of the villa's most interesting features is the fresco cycle by Giambattista Tiepolo, painted in 1757 for Giustino Valmarana. Tiepolo worked on the villa and the Hall of Olympus in the guest house, while his son, Giandomenico, created naturalistic scenes of everyday life in the smaller spaces of the guest house. The sketches of dwarves, which were then sculpted by a local stone cutter and distributed along the wall enclosing the garden, are also attributed to the young Tiepolo.

Left: The entrance gate to the Villa Trissino, now the Villa Trissino Marzotto, in Trissino (Vicenza).

Below: The Villa Cordellina in Montecchio Maggiore (Vicenza), built by architect Giorgio Massari, beginning in 1735.

building can be admired from every point of the region, in all its splendor, so too can one enjoy all around it one of the most delightful views." In 1591, after Almerico's death, Count Capra acquired the villa.

A short distance from La Rotonda is the Villa Valmarana (known as Ai Nani, or "Villa of the Dwarves"). The complex is made up of the main house, guest quarters, and large stables. Giovanni

ANDREA PALLADIO

The high priest of sixteenth century villa life is Andrea di Pietro della Gondola, known as Palladio. As an unknown stonecutter specializing in architectural decoration, he was taken under the wing of Giangiorgio Trissino, a nobleman and man of letters who sponsored his studies. Andrea's choice of the name Palladio made obvious reference to the Greek goddess Pallas Athena.

This great and much imitated architect from Vicenza concentrated for the most part on residential buildings. Early on he was inspired by the work of others, but then, increasingly following his own inspiration, he conceived the "villa-temple," characterized by a compact volume with a pronaos at the front. The most compelling examples are La Rotonda and La Malcontenta. The heart of these villas is the drawing room, often richly decorated with frescoes. The kitchens

are located in the basement level, while hygienic services, to the best of our knowledge, were hidden next to or beneath the stairs. Great attention also was paid to the form and distribution of the storerooms and other agricultural outbuildings; for example, Palladio wrote, "The threshing floor where the wheat is threshed will not be too near the master's house because of the dust, nor so far that it cannot be seen." The setting within the landscape had to be harmonious as well; architecture and landscape were integrated so that each complemented the other.

In *The Four Books on Architecture* (1570) Palladio reproduced a series of projects that represent his style as generated by an evolution of classicism, where monumentality is skillfully emphasized, harmonizing with the surroundings. His architecture was inspired by classical civilization, from which he

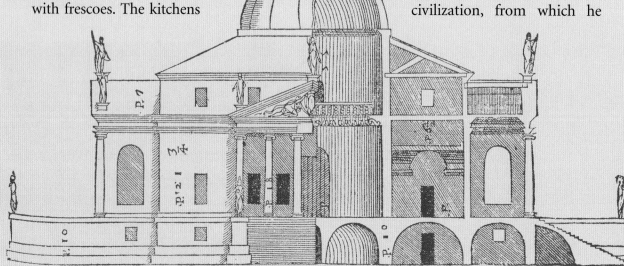

drew formal stimuli, while adding original content. Three principal Palladian typologies can be identified. One, the most simple and least defined, has no portico or tympanum. Then there is the villa-temple, with portico and tympanum, and finally the villa-palace, with a central, two-story block with superimposed columns, and sometimes with porticoed wings. In 1580 Palladio died, leaving Vincenzo Scamozzi, his less-than-thirty-year-old student, the task of completing La Rotonda and other buildings on which he had been working.

La Rotonda, above all, would disseminate Palladio's message to the larger public, which would remember Palladio for this original composition and for his other great masterpiece, the Teatro Olimpico, also in Vicenza.

One of the four identical facades (one facing in each direction of the compass) of La Rotonda in Vicenza; opposite, a section view of La Rotonda, published by Palladio in The Four Books on Architecture.

PADUA

Beginning in the fifteenth century, the Venetian hinterlands became increasingly secure. This renewed stability encouraged the reclaiming and division of vast tracts of lands, which soon proved fertile and thus safe as an investment. There was a clear need for rural dwellings that were suitable, in form and dimension, to developing these properties with modern methods. A myth of "Holy Agri-

become an integral part of the landscape. Formerly bare interiors were enlivened with forms and colors. Large loggias, pronaoi, and staircases linked the building to the outdoors, where gardens and parks were created.

Andrea Palladio, from Vicenza, was the architect most courted by the Venetian aristocracy. In his celebrated treatise *The Four Books on Architecture*, published in Venice in 1570, he wrote extensively

Above: Villa Contarini in Piazzola sul Brenta (Padua). The central element is from the sixteenth century, while the side wings date from the following century.

Opposite: Entrance to the Villa Pesaro in Este (Padua), crowned by an ornate pediment.

culture," the "tool for the formation of the true man," was fundamental for the dissemination of villa culture. The marriage of these factors and the spread of the rural and solitary vacation house, an ideal escape from the city and a way to experience nature, resulted in sublime architectural complexes, for the most part still visible today. These were meant to celebrate the owners' respectability and to serve as a secure source of investment.

The first fifteenth-century villas in the environs of Padua were inspired by Venetian palaces, but gradually this urban model faded, along with the severe image of the castle, in favor of a more open architecture, positioned carefully to

on the siting of rural dwellings: "One should not build in the valleys closed off between mountains, because buildings amid hidden valleys, besides being private and necessarily seen from a distance, once seen are without any dignity or majesty." And again: "If one is able to build above a river, it will be very convenient and beautiful; so one might be able to go by boat to cities at any time and at little expense. . . . One should try to build next to other running water, staying away above all from still waters that are not running, because they generate the very worst air. This will be avoided easily if we build on elevated and cheerful sites, namely where the air is continually blown by moving winds, and

such as Giambattista Zelotti, or in the work of Giambattista Tiepolo and his son Giandomenico, who left an indelible mark on the eighteenth-century Veneto.

The villa in the Veneto, from its beginnings, was a self-sufficient organism where servants and farmhands lived with their families. While land extended for thousands of acres into the swampy

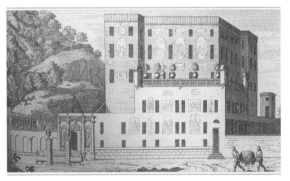

Left: Two engravings depicting the Castello di Catajo.

Beginning in the sixteenth century, plastic forms were systematically integrated into and combined with painting. The latter, by no means prisoner of its two-dimensionality, was not only a complement to the architecture but also a veritable continuation of it. It also could serve as a stage for the narration of the patron's ideals, exploits, and passions. This can be seen, for example, in the work of Veronese and his pupils,

plains of the time, villas, hubs of activity for the estates, were located at the edges of the many watercourses that divide the plain between Venice and Padua. The Brenta Riviera was particularly coveted as a site. There, an artificial branch about twenty miles (30 km) long links the two cities of the Veneto. This area had great strategic importance, since at the time traveling by river was more efficient and rapid than by land.

THE BRENTA RIVIERA

Top: A burchiello (Vincenzo Coronelli, seventeenth century).

Opposite: Left, engraving by Johann Cristoph Volkamer of the Villa La Malcontenta in Mira (Venice), and right, the Villa Molin in Mandriola di Albignasego (Padua).

Below: Palladio's La Malcontenta.

The *burchiello*, a boat (private or public) drawn by horses on the riverbank, was the most fashionable form of transportation, with different types adapted for all budgets. In the seventeenth century, the German traveler Heinrich Schickhardt described a journey from Padua to Venice aboard a *burchiello* elegantly equipped with leather seats, mirrors, and paintings: "It is amusing and entertaining as little else when you see the boats going up and down the Brenta, constantly, day and night. In one sweet music is heard, in another various sounds of string instruments, and soon another delight."

The Brenta Riviera, long considered a mainland continuation of the Grand Canal in Venice, is an artificial watercourse that brings the river waters to the Venetian lagoon. Its notable economic and strategic importance has made it the most heavily trafficked route between the two

cities. For this reason prominent families in Venice wanted houses built there, to bear witness to their social status. The banks of the canal thus became elegant backdrops, presenting the residences of the Venetian nobility to be admired by those traveling by boat.

Although the plain was still swampy in parts, its extensive fertile areas were easy to reach by boat, and as early as the sixteenth century skilled architects had transformed the voyage toward

Padua into an architectural showcase. Brief sojourns amidst the greenery of the mainland quickly became a fashionable "necessity." The season for the holiday villa lasted from mid-June until late July, and then from October until mid-November.

The Villa Pisani in Stra, built near Padua but still in Venetian territory, was clearly the most prestigious residence of all those that lined the waterway. In the sixteenth century the patron's family had owned a modest dwelling in the vicinity, with a two-story central loggia crowned by a pediment supported by columns. Though sober and elegant, it no longer reflected the role assumed by the Pisani family. The present, imposing complex was begun around 1720, at the behest of Alvise Pisano (future doge of Venice) and his brother Almorò, in accordance with the designs of Gerolamo Frigimelica Ruberti, a Paduan nobleman and the architect favored by the powerful family. In 1728 the park and many of its structures were almost complete, but the villa was

l'oeil, and mythological and allegorical themes, the work of various artists. These culminate in the large drawing room, dominated by the *Glory of the Pisani Family*, Giambattista Tiepolo's last work before leaving for Madrid. Here a refined perspectival illusionism celebrates the patron and the artist himself. The figures seem to be admiring the allegories that loom over them, while the steadiness and apparent absence of enthusiasm in their eyes seems to paraphrase the

Right: The stables of the Villa Pisani in Stra (Venice).

Opposite: The principal facade of the Villa Pisani.

not finished until twelve years later. The building was the work of architect Francesco Maria Preti, known for his rigorous neoclassical purism, reflected in this project. Perhaps a bit too cold, this villa is permeated with Enlightenment values.

Villa Pisani consists of a central body connected to two long side wings that extend parallel to the canal. The ground-floor interior has exotic decorations of a Chinese, Turkish, and Persian cast, along with others that depict the typical activities of villa life, from hunting to games to festivities. The other one hundred rooms have copious depictions of ruins, trompe-

end of Venice, or rather its transfiguration from reality to legend. The Hall of Views is filled with charming panoramas embellished with villas, castles, and the Villa Pisani itself.

While the dense six-acre (10-hectare) park, also designed by Frigimelica, still bears significant traces of past splendors, it now has the form it assumed in the nineteenth century, when it was renovated to conform to Romantic tastes. Stables, used for the patrons' twenty-four horses, lie on an axis with the villa, linked to it by a long basin. An arch with a hexagonal plan, where six avenues arranged in a sunburst pattern converge,

Opposite: Villa Foscarini in Stra (Venice), which once stood by a broad meadow but has now been engulfed by urban sprawl.

Below: Villa Recanati Zucconi in Fiesso d'Artico (Venice). Built in the early eighteenth century, it is characterized by a slender, elegant, central element that ends in a pediment.

has a central oculus crowned by an accessible walkway that functions as a lookout. A short distance away is a boxwood maze, with a turret at its center, around which a spiral staircase winds. Skillfully executed statues abound, mixed in with the vegetation. Gabriele D'Annunzio described them in *Il fuoco*: "They were innumerable, like a dispersed people, still white, or gray, or yellowed with lichen, or greenish with moss, or mottled, and in all poses and with all gestures. Gods, Heroes, Nymphs, Seasons, Hours, with arches, with thunderbolts, garlands, cornucopias, with torches, with all the emblems of power, wealth,

and pleasure, exiles from the fountains, grottos, labyrinths, pergolas, porticoes, friends of the boxwood and the evergreen myrtle, protectresses of fugitive loves, witnesses to eternal oaths, figures of a dream much more ancient than the hands that had made them and the eyes that had gazed upon them in the destroyed gardens."

Guests at the complex have included the sons of Catherine of Russia, Archduchess Maria Elisabetta of Austria, Gustave II of Sweden, Napoleon (who acquired it), Charles IV of Spain, and a great many others who have not been able to resist its irrepressible and dazzling charm.

GIAMBATTISTA TIEPOLO

VENICE, 1696–MADRID, 1770

Son of Domenico, a merchant in the shipping industry, Giambattista Tiepolo inherited his father's entrepreneurial spirit. In fact he was not only an esteemed artist but also a successful businessman who managed a large workshop. He favored frescoed painting cycles over the portraits and views on canvas so much in vogue in eighteenth-century Venice.

Tiepolo was a great admirer of Paolo Veronese, who also worked on large-scale painting cycles. But Tiepolo went further, conceiving his compositions as a function of the architecture, especially rococo settings, which were particularly rich in scrolls and ornamentation. Many of his subjects are taken from everyday life, and although his compositions are generally dramatic, his color is soft and predominantly pale, and the light in his landscapes adheres closely to realistic atmospheric effects.

In 1717 Tiepolo was admitted to the guild of Venetian painters and subsequently worked for the doge and numerous noble families in the city, including the Pisani family. In 1760, in preparation for work on the ceiling of the ballroom in their villa in Stra, Giambattista made a model of *The Apotheosis of the Pisani Family*, a large decorative cycle framed by monochrome figures representing satyrs. His sons

Giandomenico and Lorenzo also worked on the project, along with a trompe-l'oeil specialist, Girolamo Mengozzi Colonna. The center of the composition is left extremely airy, with broad expanses of sky; family groups, Bacchic scenes, and *rocaille* decorations are concen-

trated around the edges. The entire composition was created for the appreciation and enjoyment of the Pisanis, who saw their family saga recounted and mythicized. Tiepolo also worked on the Villa Valmarana in Vicenza, before moving definitively to the Spanish court in 1762, upon the invitation of King Charles III. There he decorated various halls of the royal palace, particularly the throne room, where he painted his *Glory of Spain*. As Tiepolo's fame grew internationally, the level of his production never faltered.

Ballroom of the Villa Pisani in Stra (Venice).

VENICE

By the fifteenth century, the wealth of Venice had become proverbial. It continued to grow, through lucrative trade with the East, until it seemed necessary for the city's wealthy to diversify their investments, particularly as shifting political balances made navigation seem riskier. Gradually agriculture became a valid alternative way to invest profits from trade.

Around the fifteenth century, Venice began the economic colonization of the mainland; this

Above: Villa Tron in Dolo (Venice), eighteenth-century engraving by Johan Cristoph Volkamer; right, the main facade.

activity went beyond the territories neighboring the Lagoon City and soon affected the countryside around Padua, Treviso, and Vicenza. Vast estates came into Venetian hands in various and sometimes dubious ways. Some were simply bought, or received as dowries or inheritances, while others were taken over after confiscation from traitors, heretics, and debtors. Still other lands were acquired in little-publicized auctions, or even

through the theft of municipal or ecclesiastical assets. Such appropriations did not pass unobserved; they were criticized both by authorities on the mainland, who saw the best lands being taken over, and by those in Venice proper who, particularly in the sixteenth century, were wary of activities that diverted attention from maritime trade, mainstay of the Republic's fortunes.

The Venetians, drawn by favorable prices and a healthy climate, were inspired by the humanist ideal of intellectual leisure, to be indulged in pleasurable, out-of-the-way places. They invested great sums of money in lands and real estate, creating immense estates. These new Venetian investors soon were emulating the local moneyed

Below right: The elegant frescoed facade of the Villa Soranza in Fiesso d'Artico (Venice).

Below: Villa Fregnana in Fiesso d'Artico.

leading the ideal bucolic life, in touch both with nature and with the society of his times, with its productive and commercial requirements.

The Venetians—who cherished an image of themselves connected to the mainland—experienced the country life as a return to their origins. Owning a villa became a necessary status symbol, a precious calling card both for families like the Contarini or the Pisani—the wealthiest aristocrats with the most ancient and noble lineage and for the new patrician class, who bought their social standing from the seventeenth century on, replenishing the city's war-depleted coffers.

Opposite: One of the various villas belonging to the Giustiniani family, outside Venice.

aristocracy. The poet Francesco Petrarch was an early example; in the fifteenth century he already had a house in Arquà, amid the Euganean hills, where he engaged in the activities of the "farmer and architect," one who knew and loved the land and profited from it. He presented himself as

JOHANN CRISTOPH VOLKAMER

NUREMBERG, 1644–1720

Johann Cristoph Volkamer was the author of *Continuation der Nürnbergischen Hesperidum*, a collection of engravings published in Nuremberg, which documents various subjects, including the villas of the Brenta Riviera and the Euganean hills. Published by Johann Andreas Endter, the book bears an imperial stamp dated 1714. Unfortunately, during the Second World War, the entire archival heritage stored in the city of Nuremberg was destroyed. As a result, little information about Volkamer's activity remains, but we do know that he was a fine naturalist as well as a passionate art lover. He was the oldest of five children of Johann Georg Volkamer, an important member of Nuremberg's social and intellectual elite and a well-known doctor and enthusiastic scholar of botany. The elder Volkamer took numerous trips to Italy and installed a *viridarium,* or pleasure garden, at home, where his children also developed a passion for botany.

Johann Cristoph married three times, and upon the death of his father he inherited the family palace in Nuremberg. He spent 1660 to 1668 in Rovereto, Italy, where between business activities he visited villas and gardens and probably gathered sketches for the work he must have already have had in mind. He apparently worked patiently, carrying out preliminary preparations and gathering information, which he then utilized upon his return to Germany.

Volkamer employed well-known engravers, whose presence in the city is amply documented, to create his views. In the plates, every villa is associated with a citrus fruit. It is difficult to establish a logical connection; recent scholarship considers these imaginative juxtapositions to have been dictated by an esthetic sense.

Other authors then repeatedly collected Volkamer's plates and republished them. Vincenzo Coronelli was the first to put them together in an album, around 1710, even before Volkamer himself did. After the artist's death, Gianfrancesco Costa published a collection, between 1750 and 1760. These engravings enjoyed immediate success, and the editions were quickly reprinted. In 1742 the work was already valued for an impressive sum that could be justified by the high quality of the engraving and the relevance of the content. In 1979 an Italian publisher, Il Polifilo, reprinted the collection.

Above: Villa Widman in Mira (Venice).

Opposite: Villa Farsetti in Santa Maria di Sala (Venice).

TREVISO

A study of holiday villas in Treviso must begin with the one built for Caterina Cornaro, queen of Cyprus, and described by Pietro Bembo, who sang the praises of Asolo. The tradition then continued with Carlo Goldoni in Roncade and Giovanni Casanova in Zero Branco. Finally there were literary gatherings organized by Isabella

Teotochi Albrizzi on the Terraglio family estate.

Most villas in Treviso lie in the valley; a few are in the hills and a handful in the Alpine foothills. Some are by famous architects, such as the Villa Barbaro in Maser, by Andrea Palladio, with a fresco cycle by Veronese. This villa is decidedly innovative, with two side elements united by a long, low element with a pronaos and main entrance at the

The barchessa (guest house) of the Villa Loredan in Venegazzù (Treviso), attributed to Palladio.

center. Another important Palladian project in the region is the Villa Emo Capodilista in Fanzolo, with frescoes by Giambattista Zelotti and other works by Veronese.

Vincenzo Scamozzi, a student of Palladio, designed three villas in Castelfranco; unfortunately all have disappeared. Only the *barchessa*, or guesthouse, remains from the Villa Priuli in San

Felice; the Villa Cornaro in Treville was transformed in the nineteenth century; only the garden survives from the villa in Paradiso, once composed of "three palaces." Other architects involved with villa projects in the region included Baldassarre Longhena and Giorgio Massari.

Francesco Maria Preti, the architect of Castelfranco in the Veneto as well as the Villa Pisani in Stra, designed the Villa Spineda in Venegazzù, later built under the guidance of Giovanni Miazzi. Venegazzù is also the site of the stables for the Villa Loredan, attributed to Palladio and recently restored.

Villa Barbaro in Maser (Treviso), by Palladio, with frescoes by Veronese.

Above left: Villa delle Rose in Treviso.

ROVIGO

Opposite: Villa Badoera, known as La Badoera, in Fratta Polesine (Rovigo), built by Palladio between 1568 and 1570; and the Villa Morosini in Fiesso Umbertino (Rovigo).

Below: Villa Nani Mocenigo in Canda (Rovigo).

The first people to live in the countryside of Rovigo were administrators for the dukes of Ferrara, who oversaw the important phases of cultivation and storage of the harvested crops. Only later did some of the court nobles and other patricians choose to live outside the city walls.

Much of the province of Rovigo coincides with the Polesine plain. This vast area, located between the Adige and the Po, has always been rich in water, which, channeled into natural and artificial canals, has made the area particularly fertile. Despite numerous drainage projects carried out by the Este family and then by the republic of Venice, however, it has always remained marginal, out of the great flows of commodities and people, in part because of a scarcity of main roads. For this reason the Venet-

ian patrician class preferred to build its holiday villas along the Brenta Riviera.

The hydrography of the terrain necessitated careful site selection for villas, usually on knolls or embankments, protected from the abundant and sometimes unpredictable waters. In reality there were not many villas in the province of Rovigo, although some were particularly interesting, such as those by Palladio. These include the Villa Bado-

era in Fratta Polesine, built between 1568 and 1570, and the Villa Bragadin, built shortly there-after in the same town. Vincenzo Scamozzi also worked in this region, and around 1580 he designed the Villa Nani Mocenigo in Canda. Other works of note are the Villa Pellegrini in Salvaterra, from the late seventeenth century, and the Villa Vendramin in Fiesso Umbertino, from the early eighteenth century. But most noble residences in the territory of Rovigo were the work of skilled master builders who, inspired by the refined prototypes mentioned above, created agreeable works of their own design.

EMILIA-ROMAGNA

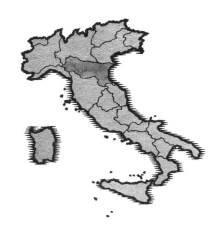

FEUDAL LANDS AND DUKEDOMS

The fertile Po Valley, while enclosed by the Alps and the Apennines, has always been at the center of trade and migrations. Long rows of poplar trees line the winding path of the Po, where numerous "citadels" and "delights" were built. The various dukedoms, whether long-lived or ephemeral, were characterized by an intense cultural life and by the centers, even now is made up of many small separate "countries." The region, ringed by mountains and blessed with many navigable rivers and extremely fertile lands, is still a center for commercial traffic. The misty plain was the perfect setting for an experimental quest for the ideal city, elaborated by essayists such as Filarete, Francesco

Left: The facade overlooking the garden of the Villa Ducale in Sassuolo (Modena).

Opposite: The staircase leading to the piano nobile.

unmistakable mark of their rulers. Today the vestiges of this way of life can still be admired in the architecture and art treasures that remain.

The Po Valley, like a small outpost of Central Europe, was traversed in turn by Roman legions, Etruscan merchants, medieval pilgrims, crusaders, and finally peaceful caravans of the earliest northern European tourists, who traveled along the main routes traced by the Po and the Via Emilia. This isolated region, a world without large urban di Giorgio Martini, and even Leonardo da Vinci. The region's large open spaces, subdivided into small, independent states, with a consequent need for small capital centers, presented important opportunities to designers, resulting in the birth of towns such as Carpi, Sassuolo, Fontanellato, and Colorno. While humanism's unconditional faith in man lay hidden, villas and gardens increasingly became political tools for the promotion of the prince and his numerous entourage.

REGGIO AND PARMA

The Villa Ducale is located a few miles outside Parma, in Colorno, the small, magical seat of the Farnese country villas. Set between the Parma River and the Lorno Canal, its principal feature is the grand ducal residence and the vast park, only a portion of which remains, but which originally extended back for two and a half miles (4 km).

Like innumerable other towns of some signifi-

already was a well-known town, with the villa its most notable architectural feature. Under Farnese rule the town's strategic importance waned from a military viewpoint, but it took on new importance as a retreat and place of relaxation.

The villa became the center for these entertainments and recreational activities, with the garden acting as theater. Under the rule of Ranuccio II Farnese (1666–1672) in keeping with the fashion

Right: Villa Ducale in Colorno (Parma); drawing for the atrium by Ferdinando Galli da Bibiena.

Opposite: The "public" facade of the Villa Ducale.

cance in medieval times, Colorno also had a fortress. This fortified building gradually was transformed, reflecting the tastes of the times, until it looked more like an aristocratic dwelling than a fortress.

In 1612, when the Farnese family took possession of the region of Parma, merging it with the region of Piacenza into a dukedom, Colorno

of the time, the villa park was embellished with virtuosic "water theaters," in the form of waterfalls, fountains, and grottoes fed by a "tower for the raising of water," located along the Naviglio Canal.

Long avenues created flights of perspective, emphasized by sequences of columns, statues, and vases. One of the creations that created a great sensation at the time was the "enchanted grotto," a cavern with hydraulic robots representing Orpheus, Apollo, Vulcan, and various animals.

In 1694 Ranuccio II was succeeded by Francesco, who shortly thereafter called upon architect Ferdinando Galli da Bibiena. Beginning in 1697, Bibiena became attached to the Farnese court. It is likely that some of the rooms in the villa were decorated with his famous acute-angle perspective. We are certain that the artist frescoed the great hall, introducing balconies and loggias, thereby creating a precise correspondence between the real and the illusory space. Other painters, such as Giovanni Bolla, Giovanni Evangelista Draghi, and Ilario Spolverini, worked with Bibiena. Spolverini's work included several paintings in the apartments of the duchess Dorotea Sofia di Neoburg, "in the manner of a tapestry," illustrating the festivals celebrated in Parma in September 1714, on the occasion of the marriage of Elisabetta Farnese, daughter of Dorotea, and King Philip V of Spain.

In the early decades of the eighteenth century Francesco Farnese had the villa and gardens renovated, using the royal palace of Versailles as a model, with endless avenues of poplars, linden trees, and horse chestnuts, and large amphitheaters of citrus trees. In 1731 the last Farnese died, and the reins of the dukedom were taken up by Dorotea Sofia, regent for her nephew Don Carlos. The following year the seventeen-year-old duke arrived from Spain, and on October 17 he was greeted in Colorno with a grand celebration. During the festivities the garden was illuminated by torchlight during the day and, after games and exhibitions by singers, the sky was suddenly lit up by elaborate fireworks.

DEA SI MISERVM SORSHVC ACTEONA

XIT·A·TE·CVR·CA

During this period the villa took on its present form, reaching the height of its glory. Later, fears arose that the dukedom might be handed over to Austria, and the villa was systematically plundered, auguring its abandonment in the following century.

The Sanvitale family had settled in the fertile Po Valley in the fourteenth century. Its members included prelates, ambassadors, literary figures,

and jurists. Galeazzo Sanvitale ascended to the helm of the dukedom in the second decade of the sixteenth century and remained there until his death in 1550. A significant figure in Emilian manor life, he was a faithful vassal of the Farnese family, a capable commander, and a successful merchant. Galeazzo brought new ideas and opportunities to the region and turned his castle in Fontanellato into a refined microcosm.

Above: The courtyard of Rocca Sanvitale, the fortress of the Sanvitale family in Fontanellato (Parma).

Left: Sixteenth-century frescoes by Francesco Parmigianino inside the fortress.

During Galeazzo's rule various artists were invited to court to embellish the ducal residence. Parmigianino worked there, as well as Bernardino Campi, who frescoed some lunettes with mythological figures in the *salle d'armes*. The fifteenth-century fortress, site of the ducal court, is still surrounded by a moat, and its current form is the result of additions made in the seventeenth century. Its structure echoes the Este castle in Ferrara; entrance is gained solely by means of the keep where, in the seventeenth century, Alessandro Sanvitale set up a clock with an alarm signal for rousing the town. At one time the moat could be crossed only by drawbridge, though this has recently been replaced by a permanent bridge. The atrium of the dwelling is decorated with painted coats of arms of patrician friends, the foremost being the Farnese and Gonzaga families, then Charles V and Pope Clement VII. The rooms are known by colorful and descriptive names,

The principal facade of the Villa Ducale, looking out on the vast park in front.

such as the reception hall, the Hall of Grotesques and the celebrated small Hall of Diana and Actaeon, perhaps originally a bathroom, with astonishing frescoes by Francesco Parmigianino.

In 1731 Giacomo Antonio Sanvitale, named regent of Fontanellato, established a colony of literary figures in his palace. But this late attempt to reform the court was not successful; political control had shifted to the great European powers, for whom the local nobility was no match.

Left: A clock, inserted into a stately pediment, crowns the courtyard facade of this Emilian dwelling from the eighteenth century.

Below: An elegant residence from the late eighteenth century in Reggiolo (Reggio Emilia).

THE BIBIENA FAMILY
SEVENTEENTH–EIGHTEENTH CENTURY

In 1767 the Accademia dei Timidi in Mantua commissioned a theater to accommodate its meetings. The academicians decided to subsidize construction expenses for the new theater by renting out stalls on the occasion of concerts and public events. They called upon Antonio Galli da Bibiena (1700–1744), whose design allowed the theater to be illuminated by daylight, making it possible to observe by the "light of reason" the

Stalls, Teatro Comunale, Bologna.

reality revealed by words and facts. The hall closely follows the typology studied by Antonio's uncle, Francesco (1659–1739) for the Teatro Filarmonici in Verona, or Antonio's own later design for the Teatro Nuovo (or Teatro Comunale) in Bologna. The bell-shaped plan flares out toward the gallery and four rows of stalls framed by depressed arches, which delimit the seating area. The building materials—bricks, wood, and stucco—are painted to imitate stone and marble, a solution that also was broadly used in the decoration of houses.

This family of set designers and architects also made an important contribution to the history of the Italian villa, particularly in Emilia, where their wall decorations embellish many dwellings. Their work developed in a typically Baroque environment, but was often enriched by personal invention, such as the famous scenes in acute-angle perspective, an innovative method that uses multiple vanishing points, expanding possibilities for set designers, as well as expressive potential for painters. Through these techniques, the panels and trompe-l'oeil perspectives in Emilian dwellings offered innovative viewpoints and a captivating visual magnificence.

The original name of the family was Galli, but its members have been better known by the name of their hometown, Bibiena. The head of the family was the painter Giovanni Maria (1619–1665), known for his frescoes in the churches of Bologna. His sons, Ferdinando Maria (1657–1743) and Francesco

(1659–1739), worked predominantly in the theater, renewing the canons of set design and inventing the system of multiple viewpoints. In 1697 Ferdinando became architect to the Farnese court in Parma, and his numerous projects included the decoration of the rooms of the Villa Ducale in Colorno and its garden. Francesco also designed the Vienna Opera in 1740, now lost. Giuseppe (1696–1757), Ferdinando's second son, one of the most famous members of the family, designed the court opera in Bayreuth, in Bavaria. His brothers Alessandro (1687–c.1769) and Antonio (1700–1744) and his nephew Carlo (1728–1787) continued the family's artistic tradition.

A drawing for the court puppet theater in the Villa Ducale, Colorno (Parma).

MODENA

After the reforms of Martin Luther and during the Council of Trent, the Treaty of Chateau Cambrésis of 1559 decreed that the dukedoms of Parma and Piacenza would go to the Farnese family, and that of Ferrara—along with Modena, Reggio, and Carpi—to the Este family. But in 1598 Pope Clement VIII Farnese annexed Ferrara, and its rulers had no choice but to move to Modena. On January 30, 1598, Duke Cesare d'Este entered the city with a large entourage and was joyfully welcomed by the citizenry there. His successor, Francesco I, a cultivated and ambitious man, rose to power in 1629 and built a palace that avenged the humiliations suffered over the loss of Ferrara. Roman architect Bartolomeo Avanzini began work on the Villa Ducale after receiving advice from Bernini and Borromini, and construction continued throughout the duration of Este rule.

A long perspectival axis, flanked by porticoes, starts at the Via Emilia and ends at the square in front of the palace. The entrance to the imposing residence leads to a two-story interior courtyard, with arcades supported by paired columns joined by pilaster strips. Inside is the vast ballroom, crowned by a gallery on spiral corbels and a charming small drawing room, where refined inlay decoration acted as a frame for the duke's private meetings.

Unfortunately the vicissitudes of the family's political fortunes and finances led one of its descendants, Francesco II, to sell the hundred best paintings of the "monstrous and inaccessible Este gallery," which were moved to Dresden in 1745. This group of paintings included works by Antonio Correggio, Paolo Veronese, Francesco

Villa Ducale in Sassuolo (Modena): detail of the facade (above); the Hall of Este Virtues (right), frescoed around 1634 by Bartolomeo Avanzini.

Parmigianino, Titian, Andrea del Sarto, and other major artists, both Italian and foreign.

In 1373, when the Villa Ducale in Sassuolo came into Este hands, it was still an austere fortress. Borso d'Este, the enlightened ruler of the Ferrara dukedom, ordered the construction of a building to serve as his vacation house. It

The spacious porticoed courtyard of the Villa Pio in Carpi (Modena).

soon was built and in 1458 was ready to receive Borso and Ludovico Gonzaga, his guest.

In 1500 Sassuolo was granted to the Pio family, in exchange for Carpi. The new, cautious government improved conditions in the territory, and a degree of prosperity allowed for festivities and receptions. Some of these were famous, such as those prepared by architect Giovan Battista Aleotti, known as Argenta, in 1587 for the marriage of Marco Pio and Clelia Farnese, niece of Pope Paul III. Shortly thereafter Pio was assassinated, and the dukedom returned to Farnese rule. In 1634 the twenty-seven-year-old Bartolomeo Avanzini arrived from Rome. Over a period of ten years and at a cost of 20,000 scudi, the residence in Sassuolo was transformed into a "delight." Rooms were frescoed with a complex interweaving of reality and fiction, real and illusory space. Numerous works of trompe-l'oeil expanded the sometimes narrow spaces, creating a theatrical backdrop for phantasmagoric court life. To the side of the main facade was the entrance to the Fontanazzo, or "Theater of Fountains," a pool delimited by walls decorated with complex architectural elements and vases, obelisks, spires, sponge stone, and water-spouting aquatic divinities.

The pivotal figure in the Pio family was Alberto III. Formerly the ambassador of the French sovereign, Louis XII, to the League of Cambrai, he won favor with Pope Julius II and Emperor Maximilian through his diplomatic talents and familiarity with classical culture. When Alberto returned to the principality of Carpi, the crowded medieval city had an ancient castle protected by a moat and some towers scattered throughout the dense urban fabric. Alberto opened up new town squares, built porticoes, erected new churches, and most importantly rebuilt the ancient castle, expanding it considerably. Transformed into a complex Renaissance organism, inspired by a unified concept and more suited to the needs of a refined court than to those of a garrisoned army, the "citadel," originally surrounded by a moat, was soon connected to the new urban fabric. The new residence, corresponding to classical esthetic canons, was organized around a large courtyard with a portico that functioned as a unifying element, accessible from the outside through a monumental entryway. Inside the noble residence, the vast rooms were skillfully decorated. The Hall of Deer, for examples, contains charming hunting scenes of the fifteenth-century Ferrara school.

A court of literary figures and artists gradually coalesced around the Pio family, but unfortunately this activity was not long-lived. The maneuvers of the Este family to take over the principality finally succeeded; the new emperor, Charles V, did not renew the Pios' rights, and control passed to the Este family.

The recently renovated lemon house at the Villa Giovanardi, Casinalbo (Modena).

The facade facing the Romantic park of the Villa Manodori in Montale (Modena).

BOLOGNA

The territory of Bologna has long been dotted with castles. Many of these structures belonged to feudal landholders, often at war with each other and with the city of Bologna, who used them both as residences and as tools for defending the territory under their control. Their castles were built mostly in the foothills, rarely on the plain, and generally on the site of ancient Roman settlements.

This territory was fought over throughout most of the fifteenth century, until the Bentivoglio

Above: In 1506, Pope Julius II was welcomed at the Palazzo Rossi in Pontecchio (Bologna), which dates to the fifteenth century.

Right: Castello di San Martino in Soverzano, Minerbio (Bologna), built on the site of a fourteenth-century fortress of the Ariosti family.

family took control of the city of Bologna, bringing stability to the entire Bolognese state, countryside as well as city. This allowed a new focus on the countryside, and residences began to be built outside the city. The Bentivoglio family was one of the first to erect holiday villas and hunting lodges, adapting existing castles. Their projects were immediately imitated by the Rossi family in Pontecchio and by the Pepoli in Palata.

Turreted and fortified buildings continued to characterize new structures for about a hundred years or so, proof of the strength and depth of the castle typology in the region. Dwellings might be located on pleasant sites, endowed with comfortable spaces, and skillfully decorated, but they retained a hybrid aspect—part villa, part castle—with masonry enclosing walls, moats, and guard towers.

In 1506 the Bentivoglio family was expelled, and the territory of Bologna became church property, governed by an envoy. This was a period of relative stability, if little autonomy. Many families prospered, investing their capital from mercantile and entrepreneurial activities in new villas and palaces. Vast tracts in the low plain were acquired at low prices, then drained and cultivated. Thus the sixteenth century was a cen-tury of land reclamation, and the countryside was populated and prospered, becoming rich not only in country villas but also in productive farmland.

Opposite: The tower that overlooks the entrance to the feudal castle of the Pepoli family in Crevalcore (Bologna).

Left: The neoclassical pronaos of the Villa Aldini in Bologna.

Below: Villa Aldrovandi in Chiesa Nuova (Bologna); two semicircular, porticoed wings embrace the pronaos.

CENTRAL ITALY

TUSCANY

LATIUM AND THE ABRUZZI

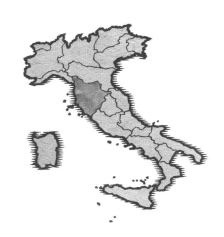

TUSCANY

FROM REPUBLIC TO GRAND DUCHY

Long rows of cypresses cut through the Tuscan hills, sweeping up to exquisite Medici villas and other sumptuous vacation houses. Graceful formal gardens jealously guarded these dwellings, in themselves refined syntheses of Florentine architecture and places set aside for opulent recreation and unbridled premonitions of the nineteenth century's impassioned Romantic domination of nature.

The Tuscan humanists' rediscovery of classical authors (Seneca, Pliny the Elder, Cato, Columella) led to a glorification of intellectual leisure and an affirmation of the moral value of the outdoor life. At the same time, strong economic motivations pushed wealthy mercantile

Left: The Medici villa in Poggio a Caiano (Florence).

Pages 146–147: The Hall of the Angels in the Villa Farnese in Caprarola (Viterbo), frescoed by Raffaellino da Reggio for Cardinal Alessandro Farnese.

families in Florence to reinvest the capital they had salvaged from the failure of banks in the north. The intersection of these divergent factors created the basis for the birth of numerous and vast agricultural estates. Taking advantage of forced labor and a system of binding obligations whereby peasants were required to provide free services, these new units of production were initially characterized by "houses of the masters," designed to accommodate the owner for periods of varying length during the important phases of agricultural activity. These austere dwellings soon proved inadequate to the needs of their refined inhabitants, however, who were constantly seeking an optimum combination of *otium* and *negotium*, and the humanist balance between the active and the contemplative life found new and more ostentatious solutions.

Gradually the siting of these buildings assumed great importance; the Mannerism of court settings and theatrical sets was applied to landscape design, using all the innovations introduced

Right: The Villa Medici di Artiminio in Prato, also known as La Ferdinanda, built by Bernardo Buontalenti in 1594 for Ferdinando I de' Medici.

Below: The Medici villa in Poggio a Caiano (Florence), built beginning in 1485 by Giuliano da Sangallo for Lorenzo the Magnificent.

Opposite: Villa Santa Colomba in Monteriggioni (Siena), renovated in 1516 by Baldassarre Peruzzi.

by hydraulic engineering. Special aqueducts were created for Niccolò Tribolo, Bartolommeo Ammannati, and Bernardo Buontalenti's fanciful waterworks. Thus the "architectural garden" of the early sixteenth century was transformed into the "garden of the senses," an exaltation of phantasmagoric inventiveness. As Marcello Fagiolo has stressed, "nature *made artificial* entered into competition with *artful* nature and with *artificial* nature," taking on values that were sometimes playful, sometimes enigmatic and majestic.

GIULIANO DA SANGALLO

FLORENCE, C. 1445–1516

Giuliano Giamberti, known as Giuliano da Sangallo, was the most illustrious member of a family of Florentine architects, sculptors, and military engineers. While still living he was considered one of the greatest designers in Renaissance Florence, known for his forceful interpretation of the principles enunciated by Filippo Brunelleschi and the ideals of early Renaissance architecture. Like many of his contemporaries, he went to Rome for several years, 1465–1472, to of his work. His most famous projects include the church of Santa Maria delle Carceri in Prato, the first in Italy with a Greek cross plan. In 1480 he began work on the Medici villa in Poggio a Caiano, commissioned by Lorenzo de' Medici. The villa, which rests on an arcaded basement level that recalls certain Roman villas as well as the terraces for early gardens in the Middle East, has a square, symmetrical plan, Albertian in inspiration. The courtyard is replaced

Above: Medici villa in Poggio a Caiano (Florence).

Opposite: Drawing room in the villa, with frescoes of Roman historical scenes by Allori and others, commissioned by Pope Leo X.

study classical ruins. These served as a source of inspiration to him, although he never stooped to mere reproduction. His interest in Roman antiquities is documented in numerous drawings, collected in his *Taccuini*, or sketchbooks.

Giuliano spent his formative years in Rome under the papacies of Paul II and Sixtus IV. He was a serious scholar of Roman imperial architecture, which he reinterpreted in much by a large central drawing room with a coffered barrel vault, which opens directly to the outside.

It is said that Lorenzo was dubious about the vault solution's design and esthetics. To convince him, Sangallo created one on a smaller scale, in the house he was building in Florence. He also worked in Rome, designing palaces and collaborating on Saint Peter's Basilica.

LUCCA

In the sixteenth century Lucca was a republic that minted coins and was controlled by wealthy local patricians. Mercantile and industrial activities flourished at that time, and financial and lending activities soon followed. Thanks to prolonged prosperity, numerous suburban and agricultural dwellings were built, the culmination of the urban elite's property investments. These patrons often gave the designers specific directions so that their villas might become effective and valuable tools of self-celebration. After 1550 the influence of Bartolommeo Ammannati also began to be felt throughout the region.

The prolific period for the building of villas in Lucca began in the sixteenth century, keeping pace with the city's fortunes. One of the most eloquent projects is the Villa Mansi, originally a modest structure belonging to the Cenami family, wealthy merchants and owners of vast lands in the area. In 1634–1635 Countess Felice commissioned architect Muzio Oddi to transform the residence, giving it an appearance quite similar to its current state. In the eighteenth century the Mansi family, the new owners, modified the upper portion of the facade, adding balustrades, statues, and coats of arms; they also commis-

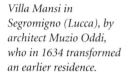

Villa Mansi in Segromigno (Lucca), by architect Muzio Oddi, who in 1634 transformed an earlier residence.

sioned stuccowork and frescoes for the interior.

Originally the property was approached by a long, straight avenue on axis with the villa, now replaced by a side entrance among the farm buildings. This new arrangement allows visitors to discover the building from a charming oblique path flanked by two lines of tall trees. The large clearing in front of the villa slopes down toward a pool surrounded by a balustrade with some statues. Filippo Juvarra created the original garden, Italianate in style, in 1732. In the early nineteenth century it was completely redesigned, with softly rolling terrain, pools, and numerous linden trees, cedars, magnolias, and cypresses. Fortunately the Pool of Diana—a large basin where, according to legend, the ghost of the beautiful and restless Lucida Samminiati (wife of Gaspare Mansi) used to look at her reflection—has been preserved. Lucida died from the plague in the seventeenth century, supposedly after making a pact with the devil in exchange for thirty years of perennial youth.

The most majestic villa in the region of Lucca is Torrigiani in Camigliano, approached from a tree-lined avenue, nearly half a mile (700 m) long, that ends at a large gate. To the sides, numerous small buildings housed servants and

Villa Torrigiani in Camigliano (Lucca); it is thought that André Le Nôtre contributed to the design of the park.

gardeners. The original sixteenth-century dwelling was rebuilt in the following century by Muzio Oddi, for the Marchese Nicolao Santini. The front façade is pierced by two deep, tripartite openings, one over the other, embellished during the Baroque period with large statues, coats of arms, and bas-reliefs. This facade is surmounted by a French-style aedicule with a small cupola.

The large park, which appears to be the work of André Le Nôtre, landscape architect to the Sun

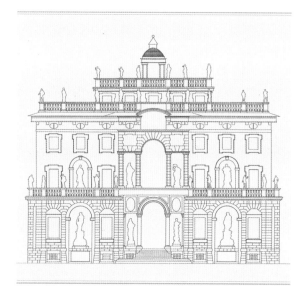

Right: Elevation of Villa Torrigiani

Opposite: The nymphaeum at Villa Reale in Marlia (Lucca).

King, preserves only one of its original features: the secret garden, known as the Garden of Flora, which has survived more or less intact. This rectangular, below-ground-level space is reserved for flowers, grass, and waterworks. A covered walkway leads to a garden of lemon trees. The passageway is located to the side of a nymphaeum on an octagonal plan, with statues of the winds and pebble paving in black-and-white mosaic. The structure is crowned by a little cupola with volutes and large masks and, on top, a statue of Flora.

The waterworks, which were particularly com-

plex, recalled the creations of Bernardo Buontalenti in the park of the Medici villa in Pratolino. A series of jets spurted from nozzles hidden amid the pebbles, chasing unwary visitors toward the nymphaeum. There, a shower forced them to climb onto the little temple, where they were drenched by water sprayed from a statue.

The territory between Marlia and San Pancrazio, which is particularly rich in stately residences, is home to the Villa Bancalari, in addition to the sixteenth-century villas of Oliva and Cittadella. The Bancalari, a sober structure with three elegant arches on its principal facade, lies only a short distance from the famous royal villa of Marlia. This seventeenth-century dwelling had long been the property of the Orsetti family, but in 1806 it was acquired by the ambitious Elisa Baciocchi, sister to Napoleon. The new property underwent a complex program of restoration, during which the building was given an appearance suitable to its illustrious owner, the chosen ruler of the new principality of Lucca.

An imposing entrance composed around a small semi-circular space was added to the estate, which was further modified by the annexation of the sixteenth-century Villa del Vescovo. This former summer residence for Lucca's high-ranking clergy had a nymphaeum known as the Grotto of the God Pan, decorated with arabesques and mosaic pebbles. After the fall of Napoleon the French lost control of the principality, and Elisa was forced to flee. Her place was taken by Maria Luisa de Bourbon, duchess of Parma.

In the villa's large garden, which is still privately owned, the remains of the original layout can be glimpsed amid the nineteenth-century avenues.

These include a theater embellished with terra-cotta statues representing Columbine, Harlequin, and Pulcinella, and a large basin of fish outlined by an elegant balustrade with statues of the Arno and the Serchio.

Prince Metternich commented, after visiting the villa, that "as one sees, the *embarras de richesses* is not excessive, nor is there any problem of choice . . . ambition and power are concentrated in a single object, so that the former always remains limited, the latter incessant." This statement might apply to much architecture in Lucca, which, like other regions, has a wealth of villas. The prestige derived from properties of great artistic merit served to consolidate and celebrate power, satisfying the patron's ambitions. At the same time the investment became "productive," improving the owner's image.

Below: Villa Colfranco, in San Martino in Freddana (Lucca).

Right: The frescoed late-sixteenth-century drawing room at Villa Agostini Venerosi, in San Giuliano Terme (Pisa).

PISA

As early as the fifteenth century, the Medici family had moved beyond their traditional banking and commercial interests to invest in landed estates in the area of Pisa. The war between the two cities slowed down this process, which did not resume until the middle of the following century. Under the rule of Cosimo I, in 1568, the family could boast plots of land equal to 84,000 acres (34,000 hectares), rich in chestnut and pine woods, olive groves, vineyards, and forestland. Until the first half of the sixteenth century, political insecurity and the fragmentation of property prevented the establishment of villas, but with the advent of the Grand Duchy and the creation of numerous hydraulic systems, the process of carving out landed estates moved ahead more quickly. At the same time, grain and rice cultivation began to take

hold, under the supervision of specialists from Milan. In the late sixteenth century the first villas were built, generally on the hills around the cities, particularly in the northern part of the region.

At this time numerous Florentine nobles

already had property in the region. The Salviati, Riccardi, Niccolini, and Alemanni families, as well as many others, helped to reproduce the humanist model of country life in the territory of Pisa. For these nobles, the villa became a new way of advertising their presence, displaying the predominance of symmetry over the irregularity of the landscape and imposing rational cultivation upon a disorderly exploitation of the land.

Medici architect Bernardo Buontalenti, in designing a Medici palace in Coltano as a hunting lodge for Grand Duke Francesco I, drew upon the typology of the Florentine suburban residence characteristic of Pisa in earlier times. While motifs typical of the villa-fortress structure, influenced by the work of Michelozzo di Bartolomeo, survived, porticoes and courtyards were increasingly abandoned in favor of a more organic relationship with the surrounding countryside. This relationship was not necessarily mediated or idealized by gardens or parks but often simply introduced by grassy open spaces. Many residences faced north: living amenities were sacrificed so that the wind could dry the crops stored in the attics.

In the late eighteenth century, Florentine villas shared the landscape with more modest dwellings of the Pisan nobility and nouveau riche class, and at midcentury four-fifths of the Pisan territory was still owned by non-Pisans. On the other hand Grand Duke Pietro Leopoldo observed that "the nobility of Pisa is numerous, uneducated, ignorant, lethargic but good, quiet, reserved and hardly overbearing; the middle class is endowed with mediocre talent and ability, but is made up of adequate, quiet people from which some employees might be found."

The neo-Gothic lemon house of the Villa Roncioni, in San Giuliano Terme (Pisa).

PISTOIA

The seventeenth and eighteenth centuries were a period of prolific architectural activity in the region of Pistoia, where numerous elegant summer residences were built. After the Lorraine lands were drained and reclaimed, the value of property on the plain increased enormously, encouraging settlement in the valleys. Against the backdrop of centuries-long fratricidal struggles, such as one between the Panciatichi and Cancellieri families, and heretical philosophies such as Jansenism, preached by Bishop Scipione de' Ricci in the eighteenth century, powerful families from Pistoia invested enormous sums in property. They built

The Villa Garzoni in Collodi (Pistoia).

elegant dwellings to preside over their new acquisitions, inhabiting them exclusively during the harvest season, to flee the heat of the city and the "closeness" of their urban palaces, and to engage in indispensable displays of social status.

Visitors are greeted by a gate supported by imposing piers and topped by terra-cotta lions at one such dwelling, the Villa Imbarcati. The villa was built at the end of the sixteenth century, following the design of architect Jacopo Lafri, who was already engaged in important work on the cathedral of Pistoia. The unusual trapezoidal plan, which also encompasses an ancient tower, opens up toward the east with a loggia. The facades are

faced in brickwork with relief, adding a painterly touch to the composition. A large vaulted portal atop a flight of stone steps accentuates the entrance, surmounted by volutes that contain the coat of arms of the Bourbon family, which took possession of the villa in the nineteenth century.

The villa's principal facade faces onto a clearing dominated by a circular space and an Italianate garden with a central pool. A flight of steps descends to three rustic grottoes, along the walls of which water once ran, offering the owners a cool respite from the hot Tuscan summers.

The noble Rospigliosi family from Lamporecchio also had ancient origins and owed its wealth

villa was completed in 1678, under the direction of Mattia de' Rossi.

Across from the villa, beyond the field and pool of the Triton, is a chapel that echoes the decorative themes of the dwelling. An oval hall is carved out of a rectangular plan; stuccowork and other painted elements lead up to a tambour and cupola. The entrance is through a pronaos with a triangular tympanum.

The project is marked by great respect for symmetry, with the principal facades rigorously identical. This scheme, repeated around Pistoia, enabled designers to devote themselves more fully to the decorative apparatus of their buildings.

Left: The Villa della Colonna, in Pontelungo (Pistoia).

Below: The Villa Spicchio, in Lamporecchio (Pistoia).

to trade and income from taxes, granted in the fourteenth century. The leading figure for this family, which was divided into two branches (one in Pistoia, one in Rome), was Giulio Rospigliosi, later Pope Clement IX. When he was elected pontiff he began construction on his villa, entrusting the plans to Gian Lorenzo Bernini, who had designed spectacles for the previous pope, Urban VIII. After the pope's death, work on the

LORENZO DE' MEDICI

FLORENCE 1449–1492

Son of Pietro di Cosimo and Lucrezia Tornabuoni, Lorenzo de' Medici, known as Lorenzo the Magnificent, ruled Florence from 1469 until his death. Perhaps better than any of his contemporaries, he embodied the image of the humanist and Renaissance gentleman: cultivated, innovative, and philanthropic. He also was a skillful diplomat who placed Florence at the center of the political, economic, and artistic world of fifteenth-century Italy.

As Vasari wrote, Giuliano was "most highly thought of by Lorenzo, who desired to build at Poggio a Caiano, a place between Florence and Pistoia, and, having had models made by Francioni and by others, Lorenzo had Giuliano make a model of what he wanted to do. He did this and it was so different and unlike the others and so in keeping with Lorenzo's wishes that he immediately began to work on it."

The model was of the Medici villa in Poggio a Caiano, so strongly desired by Lorenzo and in fact designed by Giuliano da Sangallo. This villa can be considered the first true villa of the humanist rebirth, after the splendors of imperial Rome, and the first dwelling worthy of the name. At Poggio a Caiano the villa typology is complete, freed from the influences of castle architecture and the spartan structures of house-towers and houses of the nobility. Here, unlike earlier villas in Cafaggiolo, Trebbio, and Careggi,

the design stems from a unified idea, created for a specific site and a specific patron, constrained solely by the natural surroundings, the view, and the orientation of the building.

Unfortunately Lorenzo died while work was still ongoing and never saw his dream completed, although the villa would become a model for the entire sixteenth century.

The chapel in the Palazzo Medici Riccardi, Florence, frescoed in 1459 by Benozzo Gozzoli, with the Procession of the Magi. Here, Lorenzo is shown twice, first as a young man on horseback, dressed as the third magi, but also as a boy (to the left, beneath the self-portrait of the painter), as he was in reality at the time.

FLORENCE

Cosimo de' Medici, known as Cosimo the Elder, was succeeded by Lorenzo the Magnificent, who abandoned the humble tastes of his predecessor in favor of the trappings of a true prince. Francesco Guicciardini called him "the index of the scale" that measured the political equilibrium in fifteenth-century Italy, thus stressing the crucial importance of the Medici dukedom. Under Lorenzo's astute patronage, the splendors

Below: The Medici villa in Poggio a Caiano (Florence).

Right: The Medici villa in Artiminio (Florence).

Opposite: The Medici villa known as La Petraia, in Florence.

of the early Renaissance could flower.

Upon Lorenzo's death in 1492 a political crisis, followed by the rebellion of certain cities, including Pisa and Arezzo, called into question Florence's hegemony. After the siege of 1530 by the imperial troops of Charles V, the family returned to power, at the request of Pope Clement VII de' Medici. Cosimo I expanded the territory under Medici rule and sent his armies out to guard these regions. The Medici state, which then

included all of Tuscany, was transformed into a Grand Duchy in 1569.

The Florentine court now was enriched by new noble families, chosen by Cosimo, and these aristocrats had the wealth needed to satisfy political aspirations previously confined to a local role, such as agriculture.

Around 1598 Ferdinando I, grand duke of Tuscany, commissioned the Flemish painter Giusto Utens to create a series of landscape

views of the major Medici residences for the large hall of his villa in Artimino. The originality of his technique (later called a bird's-eye view), as well as the wealth of architectural and natural details, have made these charming and spectacular views an unequaled inventory of Medici holdings.

Beginning with the construction of the villa in Poggio a Caiano, Tuscan patronage placed increasing emphasis on the stylistic development of new creations. Gradually, as Medici power increased, the grand dukes reinvested wealth derived from European trade, now in crisis, into vast landholdings. In this way the Medici became the greatest landowners and capitalists in their state, reorganizing of the territory by modernizing road networks and carrying out vast land reclamation projects. The villa, refuge per excellence, became a means to illustrate the power, wealth, and culture acquired by the noble Florentine house and its numerous court.

At first ancient castles, such as those in Trebbio or Cafaggiolo, in Mugello, acquired refinements. But soon completely newly structures were built, representing a watershed in the history of the Italian residence.

The architects Giuliano da Sangallo and Bernardo Buontalenti, with their designs for the Medici villas in Poggio a Caiano and Artimino, gave birth to a new residential typology. Their

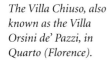

The Villa Chiuso, also known as the Villa Orsini de' Pazzi, in Quarto (Florence).

creations, swathed in the greenery of a safe and increasingly pleasant territory, would be broadly imitated in the centuries that followed. While artists celebrated these residences with a sumptuous display worthy of city palaces, ambitious patrons set aside these country places of delight for private recreation and for vacation homes for their courts.

In the seventeenth century new wars and epidemics presented warning signs of a decline, which ended with the death of Gian Gastone, last in the Medici line, in 1737. The Lorraine government that followed initiated reforms that deprived the aristocracy and the clergy of ancient privileges. The resulting restructuring of eco-

replaced by a way of life more tied to the surrounding landscape, which was turned into hunting preserves, miniature forests, also set aside for hunting, and various bird-hunting groves and fruit and citrus orchards.

With the end of Medici rule, the family's former possessions were scattered throughout the territory of Florence, frequently changing hands. Noble residences were gradually bought up by the nascent bourgeoisie and, even more often, by families of English origin. Around this new Anglo-Saxon colony, Florentine society coalesced throughout the nineteenth century.

Left: the Medici villa in Castello (Florence), one of the first built by the Florentine noble family.

Below: The Villa La Gamberaia, Settignano (Florence), known for its Italianate garden.

nomics and production reconfigured the map of power in Tuscany.

The new territorial organization encouraged investments by the bourgeoisie and the nobility, which more than ever used villas as a base to oversee their agricultural activities. The humanist *hortus conclusus* became a thing of the past,

GIUSTO UTENS

BRUSSELS, C. 1550–CARRARA, 1609

We still know very little about the Flemish painter Giusto Utens. In the second half of the fifteenth century he moved from Brussels to Carrara, where he was married in 1588. He became a citizen of Carrara, participated in city government there, and died in 1609. His son, Domenico, followed in his father's footsteps as a painter.

Utens's arrival in Italy would have passed unobserved, save for his commission from Grand Duke Francesco I to execute an inventory of the Medici family's most prestigious properties in the form of aerial views. These were meant to be installed in the grand hall of the villa in Artimino, the grand duke's private residence. The considerable novelty of Utens's representations lies in their authenticity. The painter created documentary views, a format for which Flemish painters were considered masters. Utens left his studio and traveled from villa to villa to personally survey the buildings, and his paintings were the result of this direct observation. Thus proportions are maintained, renderings are realistic, and the point of view allows sufficient depth so that both volume and plan can be seen. This is particularly true with the gardens, which are extremely elaborate and full of inventive formal detail.

The technique Utens employed is that of a cartographer; slight shifts in the

perspectival planes make visible certain elements that would in reality remain hidden from view. But these are small adjustments, made with a prudent hand, resulting in views that are striking in their naturalism. Various figures, busy at their tasks, enliven representations that might otherwise seem overly technical.

The villa in Artimino is notably missing from the Utens depictions of Medici properties. Artimino, theoretical center of Medici landholdings, apparently was excluded because it contained the lunettes representing the other villas, and thus its own depiction was not necessary. Today these paintings remain fundamental documents for the study of the Medici villas, as well as pictorial works of great accomplishment and interest.

The Medici villa known as La Petraia (Florence).

CHIANTI

Leaving Florence and traveling toward Siena, one passes through the Chianti district, where it is impossible not to be enchanted by the sweetness of the landscape. Rolling hills are dominated by vineyards and olive groves, separated by long rows of slender cypress trees. The landscape, dotted with medieval castles and Renaissance structures, both workers' quarters and noble residences, exerts the same fascination today as it did for those making the so-called *Grand Tour* in the past.

Beginning in the thirteenth century, Florence held a dominant position in Tuscany, enriched by a substantial class of bankers and wool manufacturers; it was the first place to mint gold coins, in 1252, as the word florin suggests. Along with the Venetian ducat, the florin became a highly valued currency throughout the Mediterranean basin. Pisa and Siena lagged behind Florence, which could count on support from both the

Opposite: Castello di Uzzano, Greve in Chianti (Florence); the library (left) and the facade overlooking the garden (right).

Below: Castello di Mugnano in Greve.

papacy and the French monarchy. Until the fifteenth century wealthy Florentine families produced no strong political leaders, with the result that the region was dominated by an oligarchy of families whose influence was based on economic power. They sensibly invested in lands, castles, villas, and aristocratic titles granted by the pope or by European sovereigns whose bankers and merchants owed the Florentines money.

The strong pre-Medici mercantile class guar-

anteed a solid internal balance, encouraging territorial expansion of the Florentine republic. The arts and letters were encouraged, and figures such as Masaccio, Donato Donatello, Filippo Brunelleschi, and Leonardo Bruni found broad support for their activities. Florence gradually focused its attention on the state, which had become fragmented into districts. In 1427 a land registry office was established as part of a tax reform system that tried to extract more payment from the wealthy urban property owners than from inhabitants of the countryside.

The government of the *Signoria* of Florence began only in 1434, when the Medici, wealthy bankers, led a group of families in overthrowing the rival Albizi family. At that time a sharecropping system was introduced into the territories of the republic, and in particular to the regions south of the city, already known as Chianti. Under this system land cultivation increased, gradually transforming the agrarian landscape as vast hilly, arid, and stony tracts of land were reclaimed.

Right: Villa di Selvola in Castelnuovo Berardenga (Siena).

Opposite: Villa Fonterutoli, in Castellina, Chianti (Siena).

Feudal dwellings, mostly located at militarily strategic points for communication between Florence and Siena, were adapted to the needs of the new urban landowners, no longer accustomed to the spartan castle way of life. These structures were usually sited on high ground; thus the gardens to provide for them were small, planted on the ramparts. Outbuildings and cellars were often located beneath these, or were built up against or even into the bastion walls. Toward the late fifteenth century, thanks to renewed political stability, residences increasingly opened up toward the surrounding countryside, with new green areas, such as orchards, and bird groves. Not until the following century, however, did these tracts of land attain the scale and importance for which they would become famous.

GIUSEPPE ZOCCHI

FLORENCE, 1717–1767

Giuseppe Zocchi's origins and background are still not very clear, although we know that his studies were made possible by the patronage of the Gerini family. Upon completion of his studies in Florence, while he was still quite young, he was sent to Rome, Bologna, and Lombardy to complete his apprenticeship. He worked in Venice, where he learned to paint landscapes, and in 1741 he enrolled at the Academy in Florence. In the Department of Drawings and Prints at the Uffizi. He also made many engravings, some of which were published in Venice. But no work has brought him more fame than his collection *Views of Florence and Tuscany*. This volume, printed in 1744, bears a dedication to Marie-Therese of Austria, grand duchess of Tuscany, by Marchese Andrea Gerini, a Florentine patron and collector: "To the city of Florence, which, with the many merits

The Medici villa at Poggio Imperiale (Florence).

Opposite, top: Villa Le Maschere in Barberino del Mugello (Florence).

Opposite, bottom: Villa la Tana, Candeli (Florence).

1750 he accompanied his protector, Marchese Andrea Gerini, to Venice to execute a double oval portrait (now in the Correr Museum in Venice). From 1754 to 1760 he worked as a painter in a semiprecious stone mosaic workshop in Florence. Early on he became known for his oil paintings of subjects such as Sienese festivals. Skilled at perspective, he was renowned for his attention to detail, particularly the tiny figures that animate his views.

Some of Zocchi's paintings now hang in churches and palaces or in collections such as with which it is adorned lacked a means of being able to present to the eyes of curious viewers, particularly foreigners, its most noble views, and wanderings amidst its neighborhoods, squares, churches, and principal palaces." The wealth of detail is striking, as is the definition of line, which shows the viewer not only all the architecture of the buildings depicted but also the bustle of life around them. Zocchi's engravings of Tuscan villas are still considered some of our most reliable documents on them.

SIENA

Siena's Camollia gate bears the words "Cor tibi magis Sena pandit" (Siena opens its heart wider to you), an ancient and hermetic welcome to the visitor from the capital of a region that eludes easy familiarity. It is more closed and severe than Florence, dominated by more somber, sometimes harsher colors. The Sienese, as Franco Cardini has recently described them, are "brusque and generous, jealous and pierced by gleams of greatness and boastfulness." This is easy to understand; their relationships with their uncomfortable environs have never been good, and for better or worse, they have always been on the losing side.

In the thirteenth and fourteenth centuries Siena competed with Florence in its skilled bankers and expert wool producers, who exported their products throughout Europe. Two grand families, the Chigi and the Piccolomini, dominated city life. In 1485 Agostino Chigi moved to Rome, where he

Villa Chigi in Volte Alte (Siena), commissioned by the banker Mariano Chigi in 1492 and attributed to Baldassarre Peruzzi.

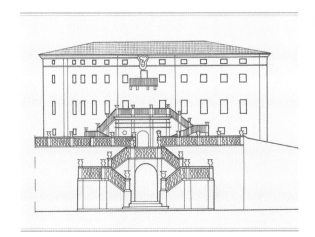

grew rich, lending money and becoming treasurer to Pope Julius II. His economic empire competed with that of the Medici, as did his residences. The famous Farnesina in Rome was so crammed with art treasures, according to oral tradition, that a visiting Spanish ambassador was forced to spit upon his butler, finding no suitably empty space.

Chigi died in 1520, and a few years later Cosimo I de' Medici entered Siena triumphantly, after a long siege. The Sienese nobility immediately saw the renewed climate of détente and political stability as a blessing for the city's economy. In a short time this sense of well-being had stimulated a flowering of villas on the neighboring hillsides. The most prestigious of these were designed by Baldassarre Peruzzi, an architect of Sienese origin who was favored by the Chigi family. Vasari relates that during the sack of Rome in 1527,

Left and below: The facade overlooking the park; the elaborate staircase of the Villa di Sovicille, in Sovicille (Siena).

Peruzzi managed to flee toward Siena, but while en route "was robbed and stripped of everything, so that he arrived in Siena wearing only his shirt. Nonetheless he was received with respect and given garments by his friends, and the public soon granted him provisions and salary, in order that he might see to the fortification of the city."

During that period, Vasari continues, "he made many charming designs for houses for its citizens." Vasari is not more specific, but it seems clear that Peruzzi's presence decisively influenced his Sienese colleagues, who drew inspiration from his experience in Rome, creating a local style that was more simple but equally expressive.

Opposite: The garden facade of the Villa di Cetinale in Sovicille (Siena).

Below: Villa di Celsa in Sovicille (Siena), originally a fourteenth-century castle, renovated in the sixteenth century.

LATIUM AND THE ABRUZZI

THE POPES' VIGNE

The vestiges of imperial Rome, within the Aurelian walls or just outside them, included *vigne* (literally "vineyards"), estates that belonged to princes, cardinals, and popes. The ill-concealed ambition of wealthy patrons spurred an era of prosperity, which beautified the city hills and the entire region. The weekend homes of Latium, conceived to reflect patrons' culture, wealth, and importance, acted as a grand stage sets for illustrious guests, friends, and powerful figures. The vogue for these dwellings began toward the end of the fifteenth century, then flourished during the following century, when ecclesiastical summit meetings used them as critical entrees to the power of the papal court.

The clergy's and Roman nobility's aristocratic desire to vacation outside the city gates, not far from their usual city dwellings, encouraged the building of numerous suburban residences, now for the most part within the urban fabric. In 1580 Michel Eyquem deMontaigne maintained that these dwellings were "available to anyone who wanted to take advantage of them." In fact, hospitality to travelers in transit was a deep-rooted custom, encouraged by the fact that these "delights" constituted the best possible calling card for the owners.

Sensitivity to ancient archaeology led designers to exploit and put to use numerous Roman ruins, sometimes even encompassing them within new construction. They drew broadly

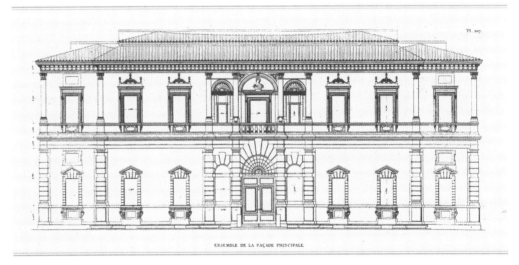

from the classical repertory, both in layout (large spaces with terraces, courtyards, exedrae, theaters) and in formal and decorative composition (niches, vaults, cupolas, apses). Villas frequently became veritable private museums, with precious collections of statues and sculptures arranged throughout the interior, on the exterior facades, and in the gardens.

Opposite: The Villa Giulia in Rome, the progression of courtyards, and, above, an elevation of the facade by P. Letarouilly (1843).

Julius III Ciocchi Del Monte

ROME, 1487–1555

Giovanni Maria de' Ciocchi Del Monte, Pope Julius III, ascended to the papacy in 1550 and remained there until his death. Although he reigned for only five years, it was a reign full of projects, the foremost of which was his *vigna* on the Via Flaminia—the

Onofrio Panvinio writes that "it seemed that the pope went mad for these gardens." It was reported that when the pope was asked "Beatissime Pater, cras erit consistorium?" ("Most Holy Father, of what will tomorrow consist?"), he replied "Cras erit vinea"

The nymphaeum at Villa Giulia in Rome.

renowned Villa Giulia. Julius is remembered today less for his papacy than for his maniacal devotion to the design and decoration of his new dwelling, which captured the artistic climate of sixteenth-century papal Rome.

("Tomorrow will be a vineyard"). But one of the most reliable sources on the pontiff's temperament is Vasari, who relates vividly how the construction of the villa was dominated by the pope's unyielding, yet ever-changing

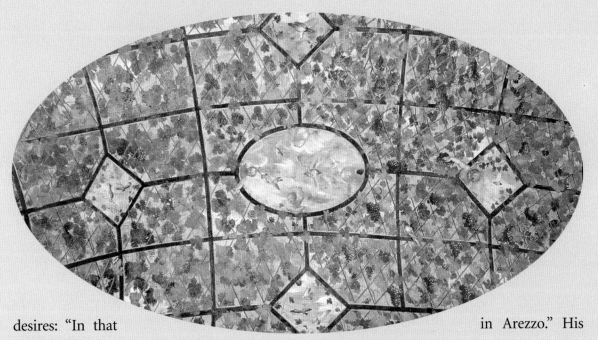

desires: "In that project one could not show what others knew, nor could one do anything in another way; because new whims kept coming to that pope, which he had to have carried out, as ordered daily by Pier Giovanni Aleotti, Bishop of Forlì." The pope "could never be content with such things . . . and in the evening did not want what he had liked in the morning."

The problem was not merely whims on the part of a patron with nearly infinite resources, however, but rather the need to adapt the project to his collection of antiquities with its constant new acquisitions, all of which had to have a dignified setting. Vasari, who also was one of the designers, seem to have become exasperated with these constant changes; in a letter of 1553 to Bernadetto, bishop of Arezzo, he writes, "If it were not for the prayers, which are my commandments, of my most great and rare old man, I would have returned to hoe my garden in Arezzo." His "old man" is Michelangelo, Vasari's great friend, who had much closer ties than Vasari to papal patronage.

In this case, too, the fate of the work was closely bound to that of the patron. Upon Julius III's death, his fantastic collection of

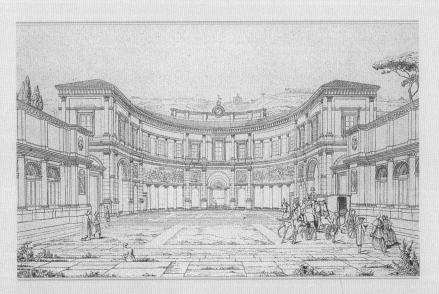

antiquities immediately began to be dispersed, although the dwelling continued to be used until the nineteenth century, when the premises became first a hospital, then a warehouse.

Top: Detail of the fresco decoration of the portico.

Above: Villa Giulia, engraving by P. Letarouilly (1843).

ROME

In Rome an erudite clientele, emulating imperial glories, consisted for the most part of the clergy, now pervaded by an ingrained and ill-concealed grandeur. New structures, at first inspired by the Florentine Renaissance, were built to entertain the large papal court, crowded with ambitious clergymen who hailed from the noblest families in Italy.

Sources list various terms used as to describe a villa. In the past the word *vigna*, or "vineyard," was employed to describe a complex made up of an aristocratic residence, a garden, and agricultural outbuildings. *Casino*, or "lodge," and *palazzina*, or "little palace," referred to the princi-

pal building in the *vigna* complex. Beginning in the second half of the sixteenth century, the word *villa* indicated an important dwelling in form and size. But the use of this term did not become widespread until the following century, even then being reserved for large projects such as the Villa Borghese and the Villa Doria Pamphili. Rural lands with farmhouses generally were known as *horti,* or "gardens," a description used even when the property was much more elegant in nature, as with the Orti Farnesiani, the Farnese gardens built on the site of the Imperial Forum on the Palatine Hill.

Two typologies recurred most frequently. The first, Florentine in derivation, is a quadrangular building with an interior courtyard, while the other has either an L-shaped plan or another configuration, usually embellished with large open loggias opening onto the breeziest area of the complex. Entrances are protected by a perimeter wall and rarely open directly to a public street. The orientation echoes that of classical buildings, with the principal facade facing southeast, for optimum exposure to the sun.

Exteriors—richly adorned with statues, busts, and bas-reliefs—reveal the patrons' great passion for archaeology, as do interiors; these, when they are not transformed into private galleries, display ornate ornamentation. A 1652 *Inventory of Existing Furniture in the Villa in Pietra Papa Belonging to the Gailart family, outside Porta Portese* indicates that some rooms were "completely covered with gilded leatherwork," although "old and discolored," and there were also "leather doors." In the nineteenth century the widespread use of iron and cast iron allowed new types of supplementary

Opposite, far left: Colonnaded loggia in the courtyard of the Villa Giulia in Rome; left, building in the Villa Borghese park in Rome.

Below: Villa Corsini in Rome.

building elements, such as glass pavilions and greenhouses (sometimes neo-Gothic or Moorish in style), to embellish already elaborate gardens.

For some time, the agricultural portions of these *vigne*, or vineyard complexes, had included woods and parks for hunting with nets. Gradually various types of pine trees were planted, and nature was increasingly subdued and organized. In 1625 Francesco Felini wrote, "Today extremely beautiful places for recreation can be seen as much in Rome as outside, such as gardens, or vineyards, belonging

Above: Villa Doria Pamphili in Rome, engraving by G. Vasi (1761); right, view of the facade overlooking the park.

to Princes as well as to the church and to scholars, even to private gentlemen, with not only extremely charming fountains, but also statues, antiquities, residences, and other very delightful and ornamented things." New Renaissance and Baroque gardens were modeled after Donato Bramante's Belvedere courtyard, which, with its terraced layout, was seen as an exemplar. These soon became places for encounters, games, gatherings, and literary and theatrical events (comedies and tragedies were performed at the Farnesina, while Tasso's poetry was read aloud at the Villa Madama).

These green spaces were laid out around a principal axis, symmetrically oriented to the aristo-

cratic dwelling (at the Villa Colonna, for example, the series of terraces was aligned with the urban palace, the only place from which one could appreciate the perspectival layout). Various elements were laid out along the main path and to the side: avenues of poplars, elms, and oak, loggias and cupolas made from greenery, puppet theaters, terraces, balustraded staircases, wide

mixed in the numerous pergolas, some serving medicinal purposes, others edible. Citrus trees were often trained to grow on espaliers, alternating with pomegranate, myrtle, and cypress. Beginning in the seventeenth century, palm trees and pineapple plants also were introduced.

Labyrinths were classical components of the Renaissance garden. The Villa Ludovisi had one

Above: Villa Medici in Rome, residence of Ferdinando de' Medici and Cardinal Alessandro (later Pope Leo XII).

Opposite, left: Elevation of the facade overlooking the garden.

lookouts, "resting places," fountains, waterfalls, sequences of waterworks, niches, statues, coats of arms, and other "curiosities." Tall walls of cypress trees lined pathways, trimmed only at the top and toward the avenues, while the outside portion was left free to grow. Various useful plants were

"in the form of a forest adorned with statues," and others are documented in the Villa Mattei and the Villa Corsini. During the papacy of Leo I, the many wonders enclosed within these fanciful compositions included the elephant Annone, which walked freely through the Vatican gardens—a clear illustration of the passion for animals indulged by these princes of the church. The Villa Borghese and the Villa Doria Pamphili kept numerous stags and fawns and sometimes cages with wild and exotic beasts, and everywhere there were aviaries of the strangest forms.

Water was always a fundamental element of these landscape compositions. In addition to

surrounded by walls so that the spaces could be flooded with water. Guests, rising from the table, would board small boats to arrive at places where, earlier, they had walked.

The plans for these gardens, while always strongly conditioned by the geography of the site and the layout of roads (for projects built within the walls), were also subject to a complex sym-

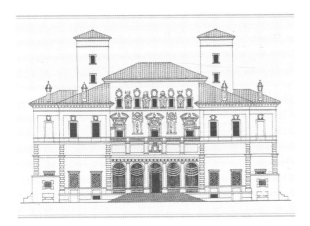

large fountains, where visitors sometimes could move about in boats, there also were hydraulic organs, such as the one in the Quirinale garden, or another created in the park of the Villa Doria Pamphili. Nymphae containing statues of pagan gods were commonly flanked by "hideaways," places reserved for the prince's meditation. There also were playful waterworks of every sort. The Pamphili residence boasted a musical fountain, where a flautist poured water from the instrument. Visitors were drawn by the sound of the flute (produced by a hydraulic organ); as soon as they approached, they were drenched by copious jets of water.

Francesco Borromini designed a project, never built, for the villa of Cardinal Camillo Pamphili, in which avenues and theaters would have been

bology. According to a treatise on floriculture by Father Giovanbattista Ferrari, *Flora overo cultura di fiori* (1638), the square plan is the representation of the "happy celestial room of eternal stability, as in a square located . . . to take advantage of the sky in a certain way." This rectangle serves

The garden of the Villa Farnesina in Rome.

"almost to extend the boundaries of pleasure, which is drawn from flowers," but only the circular shape competes "with the most beautiful rotundity of Heaven."

Pope Julius III Ciocchi Del Monte had long been the owner of a vast tract of land along the Flaminia when he decided to build a grand dwelling that could compete with the magnificent accomplishments of the ancients. In 1550 the project, later called the Villa Giulia, was entrusted to the greatest architects in Rome at that time—Vasari, Bartolommeo Ammannati, Jacopo Vignola, and Michelangelo—although Michelangelo only reviewed Vasari's design. In fact Vasari wrote that he "put the pope's whims into a design, which then was given to Michelangelo to correct," and "at the Villa Giulia he did some things without his advice."

Today it is difficult to identify the contributions of the individual artists, both because they were working at the beginning of their careers and because they were all dominated by the volcanic personality of the pope, who was filled with enthusiasm for his new villa. The exterior facade of the building is supported by a rustic order, while the interior opens onto a semicircular portico. A perspectival sequence begins at the main entrance, crossing through three courtyards and two elegant loggias that divide them to end in a fountain at the back. The nymphaeum plays an important role; sunken deep into the ground, it is visible only at the last moment, successfully surprising the visitor. And the visitor who stands within the loggia that separates the first two courtyards can easily admire the spectacle presented by an expressive water theater.

In the entrance facade to this second courtyard a bas-relief represents, among other things, the

A drawing room of the Villa Borghese in Rome; right, the aviary in the park.

villa itself, as well as the words "Fons Virginis villae Juliae" (Virgin Spring of the Villa Giulia). This inscription is key to interpreting the fountain and its theater, the highlights of the complex symbology tied to the building's formal composition. There were numerous sculptures everywhere, particularly those from ancient times,

which Julius III collected passionately. Many were placed in a secret garden, connected to the villa and surrounded by tall walls. In another, larger garden, the Hortus Terminorum, grape-vines climbed over eighteen ancient herms.

After Pope Julius died, his art collection was plundered. For a time the villa housed foreign guests, who would stop there before a triumphal entrance into the city. It was abandoned for years, then used as a warehouse and lodging for soldiers until 1889, when it became the site for the Museum of Etruscan Art. And in addition to the collection on display, the villa is interesting for its interior and nymphaeum.

CASTELLI ROMANI

In the fifteenth and sixteenth centuries the Roman plain was predominantly swampy, punctuated here and there by the ruins of aqueducts and medieval castles, and frequented mainly by shepherds. The towns closest to the city, or in any case most easily accessible, were Tivoli, Frascati, and a few other places in the Alban hills. Frascati in particular was a favorite holiday destination for the Roman elite. During its period of greatest splendor it boasted twelve villas, the most

as "wild, being for the most part covered with ruins of buildings," "ruins" upon which sumptuous dwellings were built, with some remains left to embellish gardens and patios. Other aristocratic residences, such as the Villa Farnese, the Villa Caprarola, the Palazzo Orsini in Bomarzo, and the Villa Giustiniani in Bassano di Sutri, were built instead on large landed estates, while the Villa Sacchetti Chigi in Castel Fusano and the Villa di Santacroce in Oriolo Romano occupied recently reclaimed lands.

Above: Villa Lancellotti in Frascati (Rome).

Right: Hall of Maps in the Villa Farnese in Caprarola (Viterbo).

Opposite: Villa Grazioli in Frascati (Rome).

important of which included the Villa Mondragone, the Villa Aldobrandini, and the Villa Ludovisi. In 1671 Father Athanasius Kircher wrote that the latter excelled "in the amplitude and magnificence of the buildings, the excellence of the statues and paintings, the artful structure of the hydraulic organs." These dwellings and their grounds created an uninterrupted garden with vineyards and ample woods for hunting.

In 1553 Leandro Alberti described these lands

In the sixteenth century Latium also followed a custom now widespread in regions such as Tuscany, Lombardy, and the Veneto: nobles and prelates vied to amaze their guests with the most fanciful waterworks, the most charming fountains, the most precious curiosities (rare shells, coral, travertine foam), and the rarest flora (hyacinths, tulips, amaryllis). Wonderful trompe-l'oeil frescoes embellished the interiors of residences, suggesting open spaces, such as the reception hall on

the ground floor of the Villa d'Este, whose illusory painted colonnades allow the viewer to glimpse the properties of Cardinal Ippolito, the original owner. The images represented—placed within scenes taken from mythological tales, traditionally populated by the figures of Venus, Psyche, and various nymphs—allegorize rural life. Sometimes the painting cycles relate personal and political events from the patron's life, such as in the Villa Farnese in

Above: Villa Aldobrandini in Frascati (Rome), engraving by Alessandro Specchi (1699); right, facade overlooking the garden. The villa was designed by architect Giacomo della Porta.

Caprarola, where Taddeo and Federico Zuccari illustrated a Hall of Farnese Splendors; here the very name of the room leaves no doubt about the work's celebratory intentions. The family's coat of arms was often incorporated, perhaps in stone on the facade, or frescoed in the interior, or even outlined in boxwood in the garden, as with the Farnese lily in Caprarola or the stars from the Aldobrandini coat of arms, reproduced in the gardens of their villa in Frascati.

The greatest artists of the time engaged in the

design and decoration of new projects. Enormous economic resources were directed outside the city gates to allow the building of these fantastical status symbols, which became invaluable entrees to the power of the sixteenth-century papal court. Some criticized these expenditures; Cardinal Borromeo, visiting the Villa Lante in Bagnaia, reproached the owner, Cardinal Giovan Francesco Gambara, "Monsignor, you would have done better to erect a monastery for monks, with the money you have thrown away to build this place."

The staircase that descends to the garden from the Villa d'Este in Tivoli (Rome).

Opposite: The Mouth of Hell in the Sacro Bosco, Bomarzo (Viterbo).

But such opposition was rare, and the clergy and its highest authority for the most part accepted and enjoyed the hospitality provided by these "places of delight." The arrival of a pope as guest always stimulated new embellishments and improvements; when Gregory XIII was invited to Caprarola in 1579, his room, according to an anonymous diarist, was "completely white as snow with silk hangings with fringe and embroidery of gold done in a lily design." After all, even receptions were short-term investments with high returns, and no ecclesiastical figures with any ambition

at all could resist courting such opportunities.

In 1505 the bishop of Viterbo, Nicola Ridolfi, nephew of Leo X, had an aqueduct built that, fed by two springs, brought a great quantity of water into the town of Bagnaia. Thanks to this important hydraulic project, in 1566, when Cardinal Gambara decided to transform the site into a "delight" now known as the Villa Lante, he could indulge in spectacular garden waterworks. These were celebrated by Montaigne in 1581 as a "place . . . highly thought of, and well arranged amidst the other fountains, . . . And in that part, it seems that it is not only equal to, but greater than Pratolino and Tivoli."

In fact it is the gardens of Villa Lante that are notable, more than the buildings, which consist of two relatively modest palaces of the same shape, symmetrically placed between an elaborate, Italianate garden and a pathway that winds past waterfalls along the slope of the hill. The design of the first small palace, called the Gambara in honor of the cardinal, and the gardens can be attributed to Jacopo Vignola. The loggia is decorated with depictions of the Labors of Hercules, recently attributed to Raffaellino da Reggio, and wall frescoes illustrating the major sixteenth-century villas in the region. The other palace, built for Cardinal Alessandro Montalto in 1612, is also skillfully decorated. In his design for the garden, Vignola conceived a single axis of symmetry that, descending the hill, creates a series of terraces animated by spectacular interventions. As at the Villa d'Este in Tivoli, water is the protagonist, and its movement enlivens the surrounding stone and vegetation.

Walking along the central axis, the visitor encounters numerous fountains, some of which have been attributed to Bartolommeo Amman-nati and to Giacomo della Porta. The Fountain of the Dolphins occupies the highest point; follow-ing the water chain, carved from *peperino* stone, cool the wine for those diners, and allowed them to rinse their fingers between courses. On the lower level, in front of the two little palaces, the Fountain of the Moors, a circle inscribed within

one arrives at the Fountain of the Giants, with statues of the Tiber and the Arno. Continuing the descent, one then reaches the Cardinal's Table, a long stone table with a channel at the center for fresh running water. This served to a square, is divided into four basins. Roses, aza-leas, hydrangeas, and camellias clothe the slope, and further along, tall trees cast cooling shadows.

In 1656 Pope Alexander VII leased the villa in perpetuity to Duke Ippolito Lante.

IPPOLITO D'ESTE

FERRARA, 1509—TIVOLI, 1572

Son of Alfonso I, duke of Ferrara, and Lucrezia Borgia, Ippolito d'Este was only ten years old when he was named to succeed his uncle Ippolito I, cardinal of Milan. His career progressed with lightning rapidity, and at the age of twenty-seven he was the Este representative to the court of Francis I in Paris; at the age of twenty-nine he was made a cardinal. A long sojourn in France refined his taste and artistic sensibility, turn-

Above: The broad avenue of fountains in the garden of the Villa d'Este in Tivoli (Rome), in an engraving by Giovanni Francesco Venturini, from the mid-eighteenth century.

Opposite: Fountain of the Oval, Villa d'Este.

ing him into a cultivated patron for artists and literary figures.

Returning to Italy, Ippolito moved to Rome in 1549 and became one of the leading lights of the city's social and artistic life, immediately being named governor of Tivoli. The chronicler Giovanni Maria Zappi describes Ippolito's triumphal entry into the city the following year: "Eighty titled gentlemen such as lords, counts, marchesi, knights and bishops, with beautiful music and the primary virtuosi who could be found in the world, theologians, philosophers, poets, writers, and musicians." It is worth remembering that Ippolito was not only a cardinal and a governor but also the representative of one of the major Italian noble families of the time.

His first stay in Rome, however, was rather brief, a couple of months at most, just long enough to decide to acquire land for creating the pharaonic project he had in mind. This served to compensate for his failure to have been elected pope: cardinals friendly to Spain felt that Ippolito was too favorable to the French and too worldly for their reformist tastes, driving him into temporary exile to Siena.

The cardinal returned to Tivoli around 1560, and during this period work progressed apace. Ippolito had just been named governor-for-life of Tivoli by Pope Pius IV; secure in his position, he wanted to leave a significant mark. He would not see his project brought to completion, however, in part because after a few years, under the reign of Pius V, he lost the considerable stipend he was being paid by France.

AQUILA AND TERAMO

Below: Villa Savini, Roseto degli Abruzzi (Teramo).

Right: Above, a coat of arms on the entrance to the citadel; below, the courtyard of the Castello Navelli (Aquila).

Opposite: Castello Lazzaroni, Gagliano Aterno (Aquila).

The unifying trait among the different villa and castle typologies is well represented by the citadel of Aquila, a palace-fortress built between 1530 and 1549 by Viceroy Don Pedro of Toledo to defend against possible invasions from the north and bear concrete witness to his control over the city. Fortunately the town never experienced military action, and the citadel can be appreciated intact today, with its square plan and heavy corner bastions, surrounded by a deep moat. A narrow bridge leads to the entrance, which in turn opens onto a large internal courtyard. One wing of the building is occupied by the Museum of the Abruzzi, which contains numerous archaeological finds and an important collection of sacred art.

Leaving the city and moving south, beyond Rocca di Cambio, an ancient resting place where travelers changed carriage horses, one arrives at

the medieval town of Celano, in the valley between Mount Sirente and Mount Cafornia, north of the Fucino basin. At the highest point of the ancient town stands the castle, begun in the late fourteenth century by Count Pietro Berardi and not completed until 1451. The form of the building, rectangular in plan with a central

courtyard and square towers at the sides, is open and refined, halfway between a castle and an urban palace. An enclosing wall with protective towers, which probably served a defensive purpose, surrounds the building, its irregular outline following the uneven terrain.

Continuing south, one arrives at Balsorano, at the boundary of the province of Frosinone. Since a 1915 earthquake nearly razed the city, it is now divided between new city and old. Climbing to the oldest part of the town, one is struck by the impressive silhouette of the Castello Piccolomini, stretched out along a rocky spur, sur-

rounded by ruins. The original building dates back to 1470, but large rooms decorated in neo-Gothic style were added at the beginning of the last century. It now holds a hotel, where it is possible to relive the feeling of inhabiting a castle, for a night anyway. A restaurant installed in the cellar spaces opens onto the courtyard, which is dominated by a monumental well.

Returning toward Avezzano and ascending toward Gagliano Aterno, one comes upon the Castello Lazzaroni, still reached via a drawbridge, with some refinements added at various stages. From here, one can continue to Navelli, a fortified

Below: Villa Il Pineto, Terni.

town along the ridge of a hill, upon which a castle stands. An airy courtyard only slightly lightens the effect of the massive building.

After Navelli one can go to Salle, where, just outside the town stands Castello di Genova, in perfect condition and open to visitors. Finally, a mile or two before Ortona, one arrives at Crecchio, another town built around its castle, which in 1943 had a moment of celebrity when the king of Italy, fleeing Rome, stayed there. Unfortunately the following June the town was partially destroyed during a bombing raid, and what one sees today is in large part the result of postwar reconstruction.

Left and below: Castello Piccolomini in Balsorano (Aquila).

THE SOUTH AND THE ISLANDS

CAMPANIA

CAPRI

APULIA

SICILY

CAMPANIA

UNDER THE VOLCANO

From the late sixteenth century until the end of the eighteenth century the Neapolitan nobility built lovely estates, aristocratic residences, and regal palaces. The majestic views, healthy climate, proximity to the city, and tranquillity of these places immediately made them popular.

"A short time later we reached a rise where a magnificent scene greeted our eyes. Naples, in all its magnificence, with its houses arranged along the beach of the gulf for many miles, the headlands, the spits of land, the walls of rocks, and then the islands, and, in the background, the sea: a truly enchanting spectacle." The slopes of Vesuvius, poetically described by Goethe during his Italian journey of 1787, despite periodic and disastrous eruptions, have always been populated. Major settlements such as Herculaneum, Torre Annunziata, Torre del Greco, and Portici, extremely ancient in origin, have always aroused great interest, especially since this easily acces-

sible region, with its volcanic soil, is extremely fertile, and this particular land has a structure and chemical composition that makes it rich in mineral salts. After the Romans, the Neapolitan nobles came here to build villas and farmland estates. As in other regions, *otium e negotium*, leisure and business, generated a fortunate marriage that was manifested in the form of stately architecture. At times, however, a desire to astonish trumped practical needs, and unprecedented sums were spent to build residences used exclusively as vacation retreats.

Inland, not far from Vesuvius, stood the Villa Reale at Caserta. Charles III de Bourbon commissioned architect Luigi Vanvitelli, who was then working on Saint Peter's in Rome, to design this sumptuous residence. Work began in 1752 and continued until 1769, when the new king, Ferdinando IV, spent his honeymoon there. The imposing neoclassical structure is made up of six

Villa Reale at Caserta; ground floor spaces (left) and the dramatic perspective from the garden (opposite).

Pages 204–205: Fresco in the Villa Campolieto in Herculaneum (Naples).

floors, serviced by thirty-four staircases and arranged around four courtyards. Charming perspectival views enliven the long sequences of rooms, and the palace's interior spaces, which contain a vast range of marbles, also include a chapel and a theater.

A long axis perpendicular to the principal facade of the palace crosses the immense park that lies behind it, dominated by a rigid central perspective. Within its symmetrical organization are innumerable waterworks with canals, fountains, and waterfalls, while statues of mythological subjects are scattered everywhere. In contrast to this geometric space, an English garden,

a process of successive additions—an approach that has its origins in antiquity. One typical example is the Villa Rufolo in Ravello, a refined amalgam of Moorish and Romanesque cultures in which Arab and Christian worlds meet.

Protected by an embankment and two towers, the villa rises like a fortress, close to the cathedral. But beyond the entrance a view opens up of a large garden, arranged on terraces around a cloister. On one side is an airy loggia, supported by slender columns of white marble. In the mid-eighteenth century the villa and garden were renovated, and in the twentieth century the Roman, Moorish, and Romanesque influences were har-

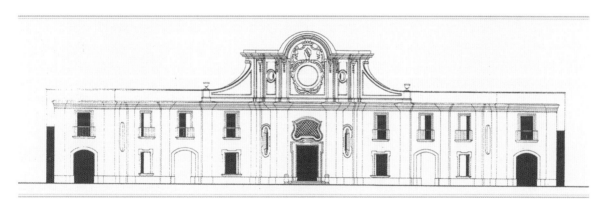

Left: The exedra of the eighteenth-century Villa Buono in Portici (Naples), built for Prince Bartolomeo of Capua.

Opposite: The tower of the Villa Rufolo in Ravello (Salerno).

designed at the behest of Marie-Caroline of Austria in 1782, has a Romantic, naturalistic style and many small lakes, grottoes, and little temples.

South of Naples, along the Amalfi coast, celebrated by well-known writers and travelers and much beloved of artists and musicians, including Richard Wagner and Enrico Caruso, buildings are sited atop the rocks, almost suspended over the sea. The main facades turn seaward, and only from the water can they can be admired. But these houses are not as imposing and aristocratic as those in Naples. They are the result of

monized through restoration work done for the Scot Francis Neville Reid.

Here, as in the rest of Campania, the green of the fields contrasts with the gray of the rock and the blue of the sky and sea, and the architecture easily fits into this context, achieving a complex relationship between artifice and nature. The work of man is juxtaposed to the fury of the omnipresent volcano, which, in the background, periodically redesigns the landscape and threatens the night with its fires, inviting both fear and fascination.

LUIGI VANVITELLI

NAPLES, 1700–CASERTA, 1773

Luigi Vanvitelli, an architect, engineer, and painter, was one of the leading figures in Italian architecture in the eighteenth century. The son of Dutch painter Gaspare Vanvitelli (born Gaspar van Wittel), he moved to Rome while still an infant and received an eclectic education there.

After starting out as a very young painter (he executed the altarpiece of Saints Cecilia and Valeriano in Santa Cecilia in Trastevere in Rome, in 1725), he studied the work of Filippo Juvarra as well as that of the classical architects, through the study of Roman monuments. As a result he developed his own style, close to neoclassicism, for which he is considered a precursor, skillfully combining elements derived from ancient art and from the Renaissance and Baroque traditions. In 1726 he became the architect for Saint Peter's in Rome, and in 1732 he received acclaim for the design he submitted to the competition for the facade of San Giovanni in Laterano. His mature work

gives greater attention to theatrical effects, a quality that stood him in good stead when, in 1751, he was invited to Naples by Charles III de Bourbon, who commissioned him to build his Villa Reale in Caserta. Construction began the very next year. The renown of both the palace and its park, however, stem less from the beauty of the work than from its extension into the landscape, inspired by Vanvitelli's earlier exposure to Versailles.

While building the royal palace, Vanvitelli also worked on other commissions in Naples and in the kingdom, both palaces and civil engineering projects such as bridges and aqueducts. We do not know of any significant pictorial works from this period.

Many considered Vanvitelli a forerunner of neoclassicism, but it now seems more correct to think of him as a designer in search of a balanced and rigorous style, who skillfully merged the classical tradition with elements of the Renaissance and the Baroque.

Marble group in the basin of the large waterfall in the park of the Villa Reale at Caserta, depicting Actaeon transformed into a stag and set upon by his dogs.

THE SLOPES OF VESUVIUS

"Even if one has heard about something thousands of times," Goethe continued, "its special qualities are not revealed until we see it in person. The lava formed a strip no wider than ten feet; but it ran down the not steep but rather level slope in surprising fashion. In fact as it cooled off during its course, on both sides and on the surface it formed a channel that grew ever larger, because the material that had melted earlier became rigid beneath the bed of fire, which scattered uniformly to the right and to the left the scoriae floating on the surface. And so two embankments gradually formed, and between them, a red-hot current continued to run as tranquilly as a millstream. We approached the rather high embankments; the scoriae fell steadily, as far as our feet. Through some cracks in the channel we could see the igneous current below, which continued to run farther down, and we could also see it from above."

The Neapolitan feudal aristocracy, which based its wealth on its landed estates, was notoriously litigious, rough, and uncultivated, and boastful to boot. Gradually as the nobles' wealth grew, new needs arose, the primary one being a city palace, which went hand in hand with political and administrative power and was a bridgehead toward new social status. Subsequently members of this ruling class began wanting suburban villas. At first the most coveted areas were those of the Chiaia and the Posillipo coastlines, where the air was healthier and the social situation secure, particularly for the more affluent families, who already were feeling the warning signs of Masaniello's revolt, a brief people's rebellion against Spanish rule. With the saturation from

Villa Mandriani in Portici (Naples), characterized by a delicate two-tone scheme that continues in the interior courtyard.

building and speculation along the coastline east of the city, people turned their attention in the opposite direction, toward the slopes of Vesuvius, which, until the eruption of 1631, were covered with dense woods, used by the Neapolitan court for hunting, and which later were planted with crops.

The protection provided by coastal towers encouraged the first settlements. Torre del Greco, for example, was built near the eighth lookout tower as one traveled away from Naples. The fortunes of the Vesuvian plain rose as the landed aristocracy invested in that area, in the mid-sixteenth century, during the reign of Viceroy Don Pedro di Toledo, and reached a peak during the eighteenth century. In 1792 a chronicler, Canon Celano, described the region as follows: "Here residences begin, without interruption, extending as far as Portici, and they are known by three names: San Giovanni a Peduccio, Pietrabianca, and Portici, which seem joined into one magnificant and extremely charming city."

Two typologies recur in the plains region and on the slopes of Vesuvius. The first and more ancient underscores the aspect of land production, resulting in villa-farm estates, comfortable, but clearly not suited for worldly social life. One such example is the Villa Bifulco in Terzigno, at the foot of the volcano on a particularly fertile embankment. In these cases the main house generally has windows and loggias opening onto the best view. A large rustic courtyard is surrounded by outbuildings (storerooms, stables, servants' quarters). The courtyard is the pivotal point for this composition, and it has blind arches, balconies supported

Left: The grand staircase of the Villa Campolieto in Herculaneum (Naples).

Below: Main facade of the Villa Figliola in San Sebastiano al Vesuvio (Naples); the chapel is crowned by a bell gable.

by small barrel vaults, and various large corbels that emphasize the design elements.

The second typology, which developed predominantly in the eighteenth century, is the villa as a vacation dwelling, usually in an agreeable setting. The main body of the building is several stories tall, aligned with the street in front; it also often has two side wings. These enclose a space generally used as a garden, which in turn faces onto the cultivated fields behind, separated from them by a wall. The main entrance leads to an

Below, left: Engraving, View of the Villa Reale of Portici as seen from the sea, by Giovanni Gravier, in the Villa Reale in Portici (Naples); below, right: detail of the entrance.

neurial, and professional classes (magistrates, bankers, ship owners, and merchants) had liquid assets equal to or greater than those of the nobles. They launched into an unequally weighted competition for magnificence, although they lacked the sophistication of earlier patrons.

In particular, this new, practical-minded clientele did not pay much attention to the garden, which would not reach its high point until the eighteenth century. The use of ornamental plants was introduced very gradually; as dwellings became more

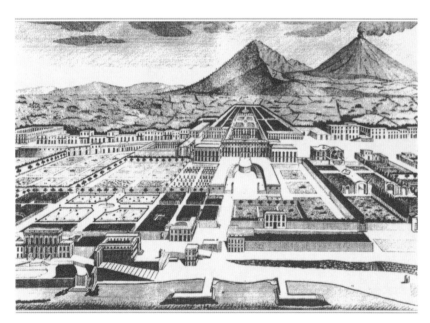

atrium and then to a large vestibule that connects to the courtyard-garden behind.

The Villa Reale in Portici represented a change in direction and a leap in quality in the construction of villas in the region. The grand scale, the stateliness, and sumptuousness of the building influenced designers and patrons, who could no longer ignore specific symbolic connotations. The aristocracy was now joined by a new type of patron. Members of the ruling class, entrepre-

prestigious, gardens also expanded. Considerable importance was given to orchards, which in this region traditionally were profuse with cherries, figs, apricots, peaches, and grapes, all of which had been appreciated and widely cultivated as early as Roman times. The green spaces that surrounded these dwellings thus sometimes appeared as interpenetrating areas of fruit-bearing and decorative trees. This combination was symbolic, for these estates were management centers for landholdings, places of repose and entertainment, but always tied to the land, a source (if not the principal source) of wealth for most property owners.

After the departure of Charles de Bourbon for Madrid, and until the post-Napoleonic restoration, the ascent of the modern bourgeois entrepreneurs intensified. They did not renew the splendors of the eighteenth century, however, and indeed they allowed great residences to decline, since these were excessively costly to maintain, and this new rising class preferred dwellings on a more modest scale.

Frescoes by Vincenzo Re and Crescenzo Gamba in the antechamber of the second floor of the Villa Reale in Portici (Naples).

CAPRI

A ROMANTIC HAVEN

Even in Roman imperial times, Capri was a privileged destination, and in the nineteenth century the island gained a reputation as an elitist and libertine haven for intellectual and worldly circles. Patrons and designers, freed from formulas and restrictions, indulged themselves in the creation of highly unusual museum-dwellings and improbable tower-castles.

"**W**ith equally rapt attention we watched the transition from evening to night. Ahead of us Capri was now in total darkness. The cloud above Vesuvius and its trail began to glow, and the longer we looked the brighter it grew, till a considerable part of the sky was lit up as if by summer lightning." This is how Goethe, traveling by boat in the vicinity of the island, on May 16, 1787, described one of its famed sunsets.

Thanks to the interest of numerous and talented foreigners, Capri gained a reputation as a

Villa Solitaria, Capri.

Romantic sanctuary and an elitist vacation destination where the ancient pursuit of intellectual *otium*, theorized in the Renaissance, could be revived. The first to take advantage of this rarefied retreat were the Germans, who then were followed by Scandinavians, English, Americans, Russians, and finally Japanese. Transgressive passions and eccentric personalities combined with the decadent culture of the early German community, turning the island into a theatrical play-

position also made it a military stronghold, which is why a lookout tower was later added to the house.

The public areas of the villa were large and richly decorated, while the private quarters were more modest in scale and austere in tone. A loggia 200 feet (80 m) long, almost entirely in a straight line and equipped with seats for resting, connected the large, apse-shaped lookout with a

Right: An elegant dwelling in Capri, built from typical island stone.

Opposite: Villa Damecuta on Capri, originally one of the twelve villas belonging to Emperor Tiberius.

ground for both exhibitionists and recluses, depending on individual needs.

Capri's special charm had been known for some time. Despite a lack of good roads, the Romans favored the island as a holiday retreat, their imperial litters frequently becoming entangled in the blackberry bushes. One of the most well known Roman dwellings was the grand and luxurious Villa Damecuta, situated on the northwestern tip of the island, halfway along the coast between Mount Solaro and the Blue Grotto. Its geographic

private area that juts out over the sea, where the medieval tower stands today. During excavation work, a finely worked marble bust of Narcissus was unearthed here.

The dwelling, perhaps originally dating to the Augustan era and later renovated, was one of twelve villas belonging to the emperor Tiberius, who ruled from here. It was abandoned in A.D. 79, in conjunction with the catastrophic eruption of Vesuvius, which destroyed Pompeii and Herculaneum.

CAPRI AND ANACAPRI

After the Roman era Capri remained relatively tranquil until, in the nineteenth century, the northern European intelligentsia discovered the island. The architectural lexicon that emerged from the amalgamation of these heterogeneous influences was extremely adaptable, as exemplified by the Villa San Michele in Anacapri. Conceived by the Swedish physician Axel Munthe, the villa still represents the highest expression of "Northern Romantic decadence." This style successfully merged with the owners' archaeological interests, seen in the way they used plundered materials such as columns, busts, bas-reliefs, vases, and inscriptions, reinventing their functions, which more often than not ended up being purely ornamental.

At the end of his life Munthe could no longer tolerate light, due to an eye malady; he withdrew to Torre di Materita, an imposing tower, part of an ancient castle that was renovated at that time in neo-Gothic taste, with mullioned windows, and improbable vaulted crenellation. From the large terrace overlooking the complex, one could see uninterruptedly as far as the Tyrrhenian Sea.

Following the example of Munthe's celebrated villa, another eclectic building was built in Anacapri at the turn of the century. This was the Casa Rossa, home of an American colonel, Mac Kowen, known for having conducted the first archaeological excavations in the Blue Grotto. The residence encompasses an old so-called Aragonese tower, where it is said the women of Anacapri were shut in by their husbands when they went off to work in Naples. The villa, laid out around a porticoed courtyard, fuses many different styles.

Only the Villa Fersen, located on the Via di Tiberio, beneath the ruins of the imperial Villa Jovis, has a unified style. It can be described as Art Nouveau, characterized by a sedate colonnade and an airy facade with a long balcony.

Charles Caryl Coleman, a well-known American painter in the early years of the twentieth century, owned an olive grove on the carriage road that

went from the port of Capri to Marina Piccola. The land was sold in 1920 to the nobleman Mario Astarita, who had a vacation home built there. The project takes advantage of the grade of the rocky terrain, with three floors that descend the ridge, from the public road down to a bridlepath directly to the sea. Years ago the current owner, Baron Alberto Lieto, nephew of Astarita, commissioned

Antonio Palumbo, a well-known expert on Capri gardens, to reconfigure the stretch of the slope attached to the house. They exclusively used materials native to the island and Mediterranean flora, such as caper and strawberry bushes, juniper, lavender, agave, myrtle, and night-blooming jasmine, which flowers only in darkness. The result is a delightful garden with solitary hideaways, spaces

for repose, grottoes, fountains, and statues, later embellished with Roman finds and medieval pots.

Punto Fasullo, on the island's west side, is the setting for the Villa Malaparte, designed by Adalberto Libera in 1939–1941 for the famous Tuscan writer Curzio Malaparte. The villa's spare and essential lines perfectly penetrate the spur of rock on which it is sited. The austere volume is characterized by a few elements: the large staircase, the curved windscreen on the solarium-roof, the plain openings of the windows.

In its simplicity, this brick-red prism shape seems like some sort of spaceship that has landed from who knows what planet. It bewitches, proof that Capri, with its lure, its history, its uniqueness, once again has hit the mark.

Opposite: Villa San Michele, Anacapri.

Below: Villa Malaparte, Capri.

AXEL MUNTHE

STOCKHOLM, 1857–1949

The Swedish physician Axel Munthe disembarked on Capri for the first time at the age of nineteen, in 1876, and was immediately fascinated by the island. He returned numerous times until, twenty years after that first encounter, he purchased the ruins of the ancient chapel of San Michele and the surrounding vineyard, as well as a rustic house. Beginning in 1896 Munthe transformed

Villa San Michele in Anacapri; right, the lookout, covered with a pergola, is Roman in origin; opposite, a corner of the courtyard.

these preexisting elements into an eclectic villa in the "Romantic-Saracen" style. The house is sited on a terrace at the bottom of a Greco-Roman staircase that leads up from Marina Grande to Anacapri.

Munthe, an original character, expended considerable energy and time on his attempt to create a romantic and decadent Caprese myth. In *The Story of San Michele* Munthe alters reality, adding imaginary details. For example, the doctor claims that in a dream he saw the red granite sphinx, now located in the villa's garden, amid the ruins of a Roman villa, then later tracked the sphinx down in Calabria, from where he had it brought to Capri.

The villa is a succession of spaces, apparently arranged by chance, a potpourri of infinite styles and periods, without any definite order, and with the sole goal of evoking a past treasured by the client. Munthe has a story to tell of each object's discovery, tales as adventurous as they are unreliable.

Munthe's intention to create a myth of a bucolic and archaeological existence, native to Capri, might be questionable, but his book's success was not. It became a best-seller and inspired many of his contemporaries. In part thanks to this work, Capri was transformed into a romantic retreat, particularly favored by northerners in search of sun, sea, the classical world, and an almost rustic spontaneity, which transformed the island into a fashionable destination. Thus it is also due to this enterprising and unorthodox physician that the island has assumed its present-day atmosphere.

APULIA

FARMLAND ESTATES AND OLIVE PRESSES

Throughout Apulia, but particularly in the region of Monopoli, numerous farm estates lie between the coast and the hills of the hinterland. These charming agricultural complexes, a refined evolution of the coastal towers, were crucial factors in the productive development of the area.

In Italy an estate of this type is known as a *masseria*, a word derived from the Latin *massae* or *massaricuus*, which refers to privately owned lands furnished with masonry shelters. These estates date back to feudal times, although they reached the high point of their development in the sixteenth and seventeenth centuries. Their model can be identified in abbeys that availed themselves of a territorial organization and similar agricultural production.

For builders, the most important issues were to provide security and a water supply. The former was handled with towers, drawbridges, walls, embrasures, and watchtowers. Water, which was quite scarce in this region, was in part brought up from wells and in part collected from rainwater. With this in mind, buildings' roofs were flat, slightly sloped toward a point of collection, and waterproofed. From there, water was sent into cisterns located below ground level.

The visual unity of the entire complex was obtained through the use of color (generally white) or building material, left exposed to view. Tufa, a local limestone, was the most commonly employed material, cut at the quarry into blocks and then divided into slabs. The arrangement of the spatial volumes around the main house, generally forming an enclosed square, also contributed to the formal quality of the architecture.

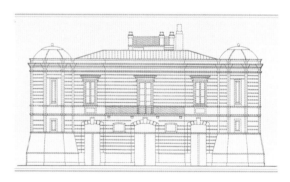

La Torretta in Putignano (Bari).

Beginning in the eighteenth century, when the economic and social importance of the *masserie* had long been consolidated and the territory had become relatively secure, some of these estates were transformed into elegant and comfortable vacation dwellings. They never took advantage of gardens or large open spaces, but they did incorporate simple loggias and some interior decoration.

BARI AND SALENTO

The estates in the Bari hinterlands and in Salento can be classified using various criteria. One is production; these properties produced olives, wheat, and grapes, or were dedicated to raising livestock. Another criterion is architectural typology: fortification, country villa, *trulli* structures, and so on. The fortified structure was the most common type and had several variations. It could be defined as a tower-farmhouse (if the tower characterized the entire complex), a farmhouse with tower (when the tower was modest in size), a farmhouse with enclosure (when the main house

The simple facade of the eighteenth-century Villa Monterosso in Monopoli (Bari).

had outbuildings arranged to form a courtyard and lacked other fortifications), or a farmhouse-castle (of greater size than the tower-farmhouse, with a more complex organization).

Every farmhouse estate—whether administered by lay or church figures—was a self-sufficient organism, containing within its precinct a church, a mill, an oven, a press, farmworkers' houses, storerooms, stables, a chicken house, a dovecote, and various workshops. The central core of the complex was a quadrangular, multi-storied building equipped with a drawbridge,

sliding gates, a bell, embrasures, slot openings in the walls, and an enclosing wall. The spaces on the second floor were linked to those on the ground floor by a trap door and a rung ladder. The ground floor served as a storehouse for supplies of foodstuffs, arms, and oil, guaranteeing self-sufficiency for about one month. In case of a siege, the drawbridge, which stretched between a staircase and the terrace, could be raised, by means of the embrasures built toward the entrance and windows. Stones could be hurled, boiling oil poured down, and harquebuses fired

the last century. As these complexes became more economically viable and the political-social situation stabilized, wealthy property owners refined these spartan dwellings, which were sometimes used only as vacation houses, as an alternative to city palaces. Some were transformed into veritable villas, while others were simply made more comfortable. Areas used by the owners were isolated, separating the residential zone from the agricultural, in conformity with the elitist and aristocratic lifestyle that was widespread in the rest of Italy.

Below left: Villa Palmieri in Sannicandro (Foggia), with a cylindrical tower at each corner.

Below: The principal facade of the Villa Carestia in Ostuni (Bari), characterized by an elegant Baroque pediment.

through the slot openings in the walls.

Next to the farmhouse were olive presses where oil was produced. During the period of Venetian domination (1495–1530) Apulian oil was exported by Venetian merchants and also used in Venice for both food preparation and illumination.

In the eighteenth century Apulian farmhouses became more open and comfortable, although their fortified aspect was preserved and certain defensive elements remained indispensable until

MONOPOLI

At the beginning of the sixteenth century, during the period of Venetian domination, the ancient town of Monopoli, on the coast between Bari and Brindisi, became an important center of olive oil production. During this period defense and control of the region, still subject to incursions of brigands and pirates, gradually passed from castles and coastal towers to the nascent farm estates. The new complexes more successfully united

Above: Villa Caramanna in Monopoli (Bari).

Right: Villa San Domenico in Savelletri di Fasano (Brindisi), recently renovated and now a hotel.

defensive functions with those of agricultural production, necessary for meeting the growing need for products. These estates were organized around vast, laboriously cultivated plots of land.

Farm estates soon became centers of social as well as agricultural life, where production (mainly olives, grapes, and almonds) was planned and rationalized, and crops harvested and readied for market.

The fortified estates of the Monopoli region, some of the earliest examples of organized farming enterprises in Italy, strengthened and institutionalized man's presence in vast areas, in practice

replacing the central administrative power of the territory and serving as a visual and economic point of reference for farmworkers. In some cases one can still see a Byzantine cross with the letters HIS (*Iesus Hominum Salvator*), the sign of the farm estates of the large, powerful monasteries of Monopoli and Conversanto. Other no less beautiful and equally numerous estates belonged to wealthy laypersons and to the local nobility, which had decided to take advantage of the extensive properties that they had owned for centuries.

These new communities flourished chiefly along the coast and on the hilltops between Monopoli, Ostuni, and Putigliano. In the seventeenth century the network of farm estates was so widespread that a distinctive typology evolved,

Above: A noble coat of arms on the facade of Villa Conchia in Monopoli (Bari).

Right: Fortified entrance to the farm buildings of Villa Santissima in Turi (Bari).

resulting in charming architectural complexes that still can be seen today.

The original and principal core seems to have been derived from the coastal lookout tower, with its square plan, articulated on two floors, and the characteristic steep, narrow staircase, with a single or double ramp, ending at a drawbridge (now masonry), which leads to the second floor. In the earliest and most spartan examples, this second floor consists of a large, simple space with a chimney, used as a living room kitchen. The ground floor, originally equipped only with small openings thirteen to sixteen feet (4 to 5 m) above floor level, was accessed from the upper floor through a trapdoor and movable rung ladder. This space was used to store foodstuffs and

arms, allowing self-sufficiency for several weeks. The terrace, like the mezzanine, was reached by a single-ramp staircase cut into the wall.

In some cases there were watchtowers for sentinels, while the various openings were frequently protected by arrow slits and embrasures, located on the terrace parapet. Below ground level a cistern collected rainwater from terra-cotta channels set into the stone masonry. Sometimes there also was a basement, frequently excavated from the tufa, where olives were pressed.

Castello Marchione in Conversano (Bari), an ancient castle that was transformed into an aristocratic residence in the late seventeenth century by Giulio Antonio Acquaviva of Aragon, duke of Atri and count of Conversano.

SICILY

A Cosmopolitan Land

During the period of Arab rule the picturesque Palermitan plan already boasted some splendid villas, set within luxurious tropical gardens, for the most part set aside for the private recreation of the sovereigns. Their magnificence was such that Ibn Gubayr, an Arab traveler from Spain, exclaimed during a visit in 1184 that "the palaces of the king encircle the throat of the city like necklaces around the neck of full-breasted maidens."

With the death of Federico II, central power in Sicily passed to the barons of the aristocracy, who gradually left their inland castles and fortresses to move to the lively capital; in a renewed climate of security and relative well-being, they became increasingly refined. Many of these families were not of noble origins; their wealth, based on the *ius coltivandi* (the right to acquire uncultivated lands) and on the *ius aedificandi* (the right to build upon those lands), enabled them to acquire noble titles and pursue social status.

Villas did not always start out as such, and numerous simpler dwellings were transformed from strictly agricultural, often fortified structures into elegant vacation homes. The newfound security of the territory led to the renovation of these buildings, with the transformation or refinement of walls, towers, and crenelated fortifications.

In the seventeenth and eighteenth centuries the tranquil Piana dei Colli between Palermo and Mondello saw unrestrained activity. Nobles and large landowners competed frantically and ostentatiously to create the most beautiful and spectacular villa or garden. Once-humble structures were embellished with tympanums, pediments, portals, and balustrades. But the star attraction in every renovation was always the grand staircase.

Access to the piano nobile represented the social climbing of patrons, who squandered their possessions in the frivolous yearning to outdo the competition.

In the region of Siracusa, beginning in the eighteenth century, the great estates were divided up, and farm estates came into being. Vast complexes grouped together the main dwelling, farmers' cottages, and rural houses into a single compact and well-equipped organism. During the subsequent century, in Catania, along the Viale Regina Margherita, elegant neoclassical residences multiplied, surrounded by gardens dense with palm trees and cactus plants.

Above: In Sicily the courtyards and gardens intersect and merge, creating shadowy spaces set aside as areas of repose for the noble proprietors.

Opposite: Villa Palagonia in Bagheria (Palermo).

TRAPANI

In the twelfth century, during the reign of Ruggero II, the Arab geographer al-Idrisi wrote that "no castle has a stronger site or better construction" than the one in Castellammare, between Palermo and Trapani. Over time the impressive fortification appeared less gloomy and more consistent with the residence of a gentleman, and fishermen's houses appeared on its ramparts. Some of these were later embellished with coats of arms and other decorations, as they became residences for the nobility and powerful figures in the region. One such dwelling is the Villa Safina. Spread out upon the delightful terrace, recently restored to its original elegance by Maria Randazzo, the villa overlooks the legendary "queen's pool," an inlet where it is said an extremely beautiful châtelaine used to bathe among the most exotic fish. According to the

The eclectic twentieth-century facade of the Villa Elena in Valderice (Trapani).

legend, one day the noblewoman, tormented by love, committed suicide, jumping from the top of the tower into this pool.

Several miles west of Castellammare is Scopello, an ancient seaside town said to have been built on the ruins of the mythical Cetaria, "City of Tuna." This lovely creek is the site of two lookout towers. One, from the thirteenth century, is now in ruins; the other, from the late sixteenth century, known

dwellings, and farm buildings, often fortified and self-sufficient—are still in some cases flourishing centers of business activity, however. Trapani, described by the Arab traveler Ibn Gubayr as a "hardly spacious . . . enclosed by a wall, white as a dove," prospered from fishing, salt production, and agriculture. These centers, along with the towers and castles, were important points of reference in the region.

Left: A putto in the garden of the Villa Whitaker in Palermo.

Below: The Torre Doria in Scopello, in the vicinity of Castellammare del Golfo (Trapani).

as the Doria or the Aragona, stands upon a cliff, looming over the tuna-fishing grounds that date back to Arab times. Traveling along the coast toward Trapani, one arrives at San Vito lo Capo, located on a narrow promontory that marks the western tip of the gulf. In the town, Norman in origin, is the mother church, an ancient sixteenth-century fortress inhabited by the governor, which retains the exterior characteristics of a noble fortified dwelling.

The hinterland, which is extremely fertile in parts, is dotted with many farms, some long abandoned. These important agricultural centers—composed of a main house, farmworkers'

PALERMO

Life in Palermo in the sixteenth and seventeenth centuries was characterized by opulence and ostentatious display on the part of both old and new nobles, who competed with each other and with the court. Urban palaces and, in the seventeenth century and above all during the Grand Siècle, airy vacation homes served as stages for their activities. The eighteenth century was the period of the vacation villa par excellence. In a

tile terrain for their programs. The brilliant synthesis between political and economic power and artistic activities had fortunate results in the suburban and extraurban residences of Palermo.

In the seventeenth century the city still had a fortified military layout, and expansion beyond the city confines was modest. But the cramped city center was no longer suitable to the exuberant nobility, which wanted to exhibit its culture and, above all, its wealth through new residences. These

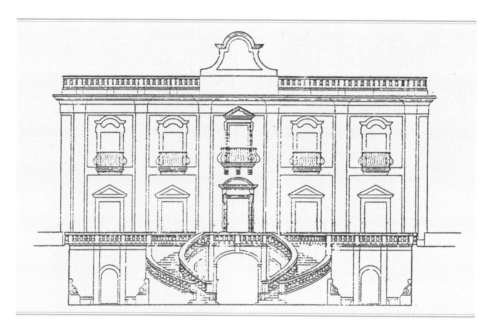

Villa de Cordova in Palermo; the principal Baroque facade in an elevation (right), and as it appears today (opposite), dominated by the elegant "pincer" staircase.

continuous display of luxury, the Palermitan elite squandered fabulous riches on receptions worthy of the Arabian Nights. Villas were inhabited for six months of the year, and the nobles moved to and from in long caravans with a court of friends, noblewomen, knights, pages, and servants. Their sojourns were spent in knightly games, interminable hunting parties, and enormous meals. As in so many other Italian courts, the role of the nobility was also philanthropic. Wealthy families patronized numerous artists and scientific figures, and academies found fer-

were characterized by a more relaxed lifestyle, inserted into a "nature" reproduced and tamed with precise geometries in dense and fragrant gardens. The city expanded for the most part in three directions, toward Bagheria, Mezzo Monreale, and Piana dei Colli. This latter region, which extended toward Mondello and was circumscribed by Mounts Pellegrino, Gallo, and Billiemi, was particularly rich in patrician dwellings, thanks to its nearness to the city and its favorable climate.

In 1798 Goethe visited the region of Palermo, and in his *Italian Voyage* he described the original

structure and layout of these dwellings: "Country houses are built in the middle of the estate, so that, to reach the house itself, one has to drive through cultivated fields, vegetable gardens and other agriculturally useful premises. But people are more economical here than they are in northern countries, where a large acreage of valuable soil is often sacrificed to the layout of a park so that the eye may be flattered by unprofitable shrubs.

These southerners, on the contrary, erect two walls between which one reaches the big house without being aware of what is happening on either side. The drive usually begins with a huge gateway—sometimes there is a vaulted hall as well—and ends in the courtyard of the house. To give the eye something to look at, a moulding runs along the top of the walls, decorated with scrolls and brackets on which vases are sometimes placed. The wall surfaces are divided into whitewashed panels." In contrast, for example, to villas in the Veneto, which strived for symbiosis with surrounding nature, those in Palermo updated the idea of the male within the fortress, reflecting a closed baronial culture that was still feudal in many ways.

Villa Partanna in Palermo (right) and an axonometric view (above) that shows the entire complex and the principal facade.

Generally the Palermitan villa was made up of a linear element, developed over two floors. The symmetry of the complex was enhanced by lower service wings arranged in a U and reserved for servants' quarters and stables. The facades—invariably rigidly symmetrical, composed and framed

by pilaster strips, bands, cornices, and friezes in yellow tufa—seem like theater sets, dominated by chiaroscuro effects and made to be seen more than experienced or touched. A chapel was often set within the villa, or it might be a separate, free-standing building. The main house, which had no courtyard, was most notable for a bizarre exterior grand staircase that led to the piano nobile. This expressive and imaginative feature retained, in its

tries, flowers, pavilions, fountains, and statues, they created a subdued atmosphere; nature was reinvented for the use and consumption of an aristocratic elite at once cultivated and business-minded. Orchards, known as "floras" or "florettes," remained essential components in the composition of the green space, situated to attest to the origins of the host's wealth. Their layout, however, was contorted by geometry, forced into sunburst

Above: Villa Mercadante in Palermo.

Right: Villa Spina in Palermo, where a large double-ramp, semicircular staircase ascends to the piano nobile, dominating the entire facade.

various forms, one constant element: the double, symmetrical flights of steps that delineated an elegant movement through the space, remaining extraneous to the facade but constituting its theatrical motif par excellence. The interiors frequently had frescoed ceilings embellished with stuccowork and gilding, and many floors were of polychrome ceramic.

Gardens were valuable bridges between the architecture and the landscape. With their geome-

arrays of small avenues that gave them an eminently esthetic value. It would be precisely this haughty detachment from production activities, repeatedly displayed and flaunted by the nobility, that would mark their decline and the emergence of the entrepreneurial and pragmatic bourgeoisie.

At the end of the eighteenth century Palermo was open to the Enlightenment and Masonic currents, widespread throughout Europe, which spread new ideas and artistic developments. A return to classicism took two paths. Certain architects, particularly Andrea Giganti and Venanzio Marvuglia, promoted an intellectual approach, seen in their reintroduction, if only in part, of ancient compositional typologies. On the other hand an artisanal approach was advocated by decorators, although they assimilated this new style only superficially. In effect, changing tastes above

all reacted against the excesses of the rococo. This had found great favor because of its infinite dynamic possibilities, and was abandoned only gradually, following the intellectual speculations of Giambattista Piranesi and his school, which imposed new models throughout Europe, interpreted in a Romantic key. On various occasions styles merged, putting together Louis XVI motifs and plateresque ornamentation with medallions and neoclassical festoons, placed on facades punctuated by pilaster strips and emphasized by different plaster tones and by tufa sculpted into the shape of pilaster strips and capitals.

Luigi Vanvitelli's Villa Reale in Caserta was a model for many Palermitan villas, which echoed the ornamental or compositional motifs of its portals and windows. The imitation was more in form than in substance, however; these villas still were characterized by drawing rooms without the convenient corridors used in more evolved typologies. This should not seem surprising if we recall that in Palermo, as in all Sicily, feudal society had not yet developed a bourgeois class and remained divided into aristocracy and commoners.

The marchese of Villabianca, a well-known chronicler in the eighteenth century, noted in his diary, "Fashion demands that everything be executed in the style of Greek architecture," abounding in friezes, triglyphs, and guttae. But this "facade" style, which negated movement, soon became charged with symbolic import, with an emphasis on public more than private architecture. Not all private buildings were completely new, and in some cases more modest preexisting

Villa Pantelleria in Palermo.

structures were renovated and readapted. One such example is the seventeenth-century farm that was turned into the Villa Mercadante, the entrance of which is graced by a bust of one of the owners, Cardinal Lagumina. Another is the Villa Maltese, one of the few that has an interior courtyard similar to that of a city palace.

One of the most magnificent examples of the Palermitan neoclassical style is the Villa Whitaker, built in 1890 by Joseph Isaac Whitaker on a seventeen-acre (7 hectare) plot filled with lemon, orange, Japanese plum, fig, walnut, and mandarin orange trees. The rest of the plants that made up the vast park were imported from Tunisia, Sumatra, and other exotic locales. The charming green space was marked by principal and secondary roads alternating with clearings and groups of trees. An immense, centuries-old magnolia tree dominates a clearing next to the dwelling. Various painters and stuccoworkers decorated the piano nobile of the villa, later collaborating with Palermitan architect Ernesto Basile on the construction of the Teatro Massimo. The Summer Parlor is particularly interesting, with its delicate Art Nouveau floral painting. A large gallery is decorated in Pompeiian style, and a boudoir in Louis XVI style. Two lions by the sculptor Mario Rutelli stand at the top of the staircase that descends to the park. The stateliness of this dwelling evokes that of the nearby villa of Gaetano Cottone, prince of Castelnuovo, from an earlier century. The large park still has its theater of greenery with a fountain at the center, surmounted by a statue representing Music, by sculptor Ignazio Marabutti.

Certainly the most charming nineteenth-century project in Palermo is the Villa Cinese

Left: Villa Whitaker in Palermo, one of the best examples of the Palermitan neoclassical style.

Below: The double-ramp entry staircase of the Villa Terrasi in Palermo.

("Chinese Villa") designed by architect Venanzio Marvuglia (a disciple of Gaspare Vanvitelli) for Ferdinando IV. The site, later called the Parco della Favorita, may have been the setting for an earlier, more modest Chinese-style structure, belonging to Baron Della Scala. This wooden pavilion was said to have inspired the Bourbon king, in a period when decorative eclecticism—already pre-

Above and right: The Chinese Villa in Palermo.

saged by the city's exotic botanical garden—had spread the fashion for chinoiserie, first in porcelain and furnishings, then in ornamentation, and finally in architecture. In fact, the only neoclassical element in the villa was now the pronaos and the porticoes at the beginning of the drive. The Villa Cinese, set aside for the monarch's private moments, stems from a new idea of the vacation house that rejects monumentality and favors privacy, as in English countryside residences.

After Sicily was annexed to the kingdom of Italy, the nobles were replaced by officials who turned their backs on creativity and neglected the rich local tradition. In Palermo, far from the cold capital of Turin, the fervor that had made the city great was slowly extinguished.

BAGHERIA

The high season for Bagheria began in the mid-seventeenth century, with the arrival of Giuseppe Branciforte, count of Raccuja, who, tested by various misadventures, decided to withdraw to his delightful estate. Implicated in a conspiracy to have a member of his family chosen king of Sicily, and realizing that the project was destined to fail, he informed the viceroy of the plot. As a result he was granted immunity but also earned the hatred

other nobles chose this area to build their vacation dwellings, creating a veritable building boom that lasted into the next century. It was even necessary to prepare a town-planning scheme, which called for, among other things, two principal roads crossed by streets that terminated at one end at the church and at the other at Branciforte's villa. For this occasion Salvatore Branciforte, prince of Bufera, enlarged the villa, adding a new facade on axis with the road under construction.

Above, right: Villa Ramacca in Bagheria (Palermo), left, and a mask/torch snuffer placed next to the entrance of the Villa Palagonia.

Opposite: The garden facade of the Villa Palagonia in Bagheria.

of the Spaniards, his former allies. Branciforte had a palace (now known as the Villa Bufera) built in Bagheria, between two towers that bear the melancholy inscription: "Ya la esperanza es perdida / y un solo bien me consuela / que el tiempo que pasa y vuela / y leverà presto la vida" (Hope is already lost / and one sole good comforts me / that time which passes and flies / soon will take my life). The count's retinue of farmers, grooms, artisans, and servants, with their families, made up the original population of the town. Gradually

Eighteenth-century life in Sicily still had feudal characteristics; the master of a house would receive vassals in the courtyard in front of the building, thereby emphasizing a difference in rank that also implied physical separation. The villas built during the Grand Siècle bear witness to this need for elitist isolation on the part of nobles, who tended to display an aristocratic detachment from the practical problems of everyday life.

The imposing Villa Valguarnera, one of the first of these, was completed in 1713 at the behest of

Lady Maria Anna del Bosco Gravina, princess of Valguarnera, according to the plan of architect Tommaso Maria Napoli. On the curved principal facade, a double staircase terminates in a closed loggia. On the sides are service areas with terraces, and the interior has a beautifully decorated elliptical parlor. The semicircular architecture of

Above: Villa Travia in Bagheria (Palermo).

Right: Hall of Mirrors, Villa Palagonia.

the villa's facade embraces a clearing; at the back, a vast park slopes down the hillside.

The architectural flowering of Bagheria was restricted to a single century, ending with the dawn of Romanticism, but its original and complex results enriched the region with priceless contributions to the Sicilian Baroque. Perhaps these are not the most significant examples from this period, but they eloquently represent an era, its values, and its contradictions.

FERDINANDO FRANCESCO GRAVINA

PRINCE OF PALAGONIA

PALERMO, C. 1675–1746

The Villa Palagonia in Bagheria was commissioned by Ferdinando Francesco Gravina, prince of Palagonia, in 1715. Work continued until 1792 and was completed by Gravina's son, who bore the same name and added a seemingly endless series of tufa statues (probably around two hundred), many of which look like monsters. In 1787, while work was still at its height, Goethe visited the villa, which he found unsettling: "Our entire day has been taken up with the madness of the Prince of Pallagonia. When a person is expected to describe some absurdity . . . he makes it something, whereas, in fact, it is nothing that wants to be taken for something." He was not the only one to be disconcerted by the prince's unusual visions. Earlier, the marchese of Villabianca had written that "the statues . . . all form a mass of disconnections and confusion. . . . The large drive from there can be described as an avenue of eccentricities and oddities, since the pyramids, namely little theaters of simulacra, which are arrayed in two rows, represent nothing but buffonlike figures, pygmies, monsters, and animals of novel invention . . . abortions of a bizarre and mad imagination. . . . He was so greatly overtaken by this frenzy, following his ideas, that he ended up saying to everyone that he had the ability to add to the creation of the animals, which God had left imperfect." The interior of the villa is no less odd, particularly the Hall of Mirrors, where on the hipped ceiling numerous pieces of glass distort the reflected images of visitors to the room, creating new monsters. The doorjamb leading into the room bears the words, "Mirrored in these crystals and in this singular magnificence con-

template the mortal frailty of the image expressed." The true monsters, it seems to say, are not those immortal ones in the garden but rather the visitors who, in their own monstruous reflections, see their transience as human beings, and so who are we, Goethe, and all the others laughing at, if not ourselves? The hall also has other artifices, such as glass panels painted to simulate marble, set within a recess in the walls, with the result that visitors are confused about what they are really seeing. The villa's other original touches include two grotesque masks, flanking the entrance, at the foot of the complex marble staircase. After accompanying his evening guests to their carriages, the prince would snuff out the torches in the mouths of these.

The "monsters" arrayed on the enclosing wall of the Villa Palagonia in Bagheria (Palermo).

RAGUSA

The harshness of ancient Sicily (Trinacria, as it was known) is striking. Much of the land is occupied by the Iblean Plateau, a barren and stony plain, crossed by stone walls that delimit fields and pastureland. The most fertile areas are the flatlands of Acate, Comiso, and Vittoria, where the rural landscape is dotted with large carob plantations, with their dense dark green foliage. This region also has numerous deposits of pitch

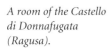

A room of the Castello di Donnafugata (Ragusa).

stone (layers of limestone impregnated with pitch), long prized as a building material.

The territory's lack of homogeneity—in terms of both geography and production—has resulted in a series of charming and heterogeneous examples of patrician residences that range from medieval castles with baronial origins to traditional farmhouse estates, of a later date, as well as coastal lookout towers and romantic manor

houses surrounded by the greenery of parks. As in much of the island, here too centers of production were farm estates. Castles had been more or less the dwellings of nobles who held political power, and the coastal towers, having fulfilled their original defensive function, became spartan vacation houses. The most well known residence in the region is the Castello di Donnafugata. Once part of the system of lookout and alarm

The neo-Gothic Castello di Donnafugata.

towers, equipped in the sixteenth century to emit smoke and fire signals, it was the first such structure to be refined and adapted as a dwelling.

Farm estates were located predominantly on elevated terrain, surrounded by vast lands. A large, paved central courtyard was flanked by the main house, farmers' dwellings, storehouses, other service spaces, and sometimes a chapel, when the size and wealth of the complex allowed.

Certain farm estates also were equipped for sheep breeding, with drystone enclosing walls crowned by stones that projected outward to defend the sheep from wolves. The region of Ragusa is not particularly fertile, and it has always been isolated, distant from large cities and the most frequented highways, one reason its dwellings long continued to be fortified.

MESSINA AND CATANIA

The humanist breeding ground of the court of Alphonse of Aragon welcomed the developments of the Tuscan Renaissance, unlike in western Sicily, where an original local style took root, not reaching its highest expression until the Baroque seventeenth and eighteenth centuries. In the late sixteenth century the Messina coastline was sprinkled with villas and lodges built close to the Peloritani hills, such as the Villa Bosurci, which is approached through a broad pergola of bougainvillea. Buildings of Arab and Norman origin, as well as coastal towers and castles, continued to have a significance influence.

The towers in particular were built more as lookout and alarm stations than as defensive structures; they used smoke and fire signals to communicate. Most of those still standing date to the mid-sixteenth century and were built at the behest of Viceroy Giovanni de Vega. Some

Opposite: Villa Roberto in Messina, built around the 1830s.

Below: Villa Politini in Catania.

The neoclassical Villa Margherita in Catania, built in the late nineteenth century on the avenue of the same name.

belonged to private citizens who lived there. The Scillichenti tower, along federal highway 113 to Palermo, is one of the most charming examples in the region of Messina.

Castles were other defensive structures that fulfilled a residential function. Castello Spadafora was built in the region of Milazzo, at the center of a vast tract belonging to Gualtiero Spadafora, prince of Meletto and Venetico. This austere square structure with large, low, bastioned towers at the corners dates to the sixteenth century, when it probably stood in isolation on the beach. Only in the eighteenth century did the town grow up around the baronial castle, wherever the sea left room.

Before the last earthquake of 1908, Messina experienced a period of growth, encouraged by the unification of Italy. After the earthquake the

or Cinisi marble, used chiefly for ornamentation.

Catania, south of the Messina region, was an important commercial center for trade with the Middle East and the coasts of Africa, with an emphasis on silk, amber, wine, and tobacco. Catania was also a significant cultural center and the site of the oldest university in Sicily, founded in 1434 by king Alphonse V of Aragon. On the large plain between Paternò, Scordia, Vizzini, and Palagonia, citrus orchards extended as far as the eye could see, and in the springtime the scent of orange blossoms (the word in Italian, *zagara*, comes from "flower" in Arabic) was entoxicating.

Villa Vecchio in Catania, one of the many neoclassical dwellings that line the Viale Regina Margherita.

patrician class emigrated elsewhere, leaving the bourgeoisie to rebuild the central city. Messina expanded, with new residential quarters built on the hillsides and along the seacoast, where numerous small villas appeared, in widely varying styles. Only the materials remained traditional, such as the yellow-ocher stone that has always been used in the region (the same that was used for the temples of Selinunte and Agrigento),

Goethe himself wrote, "Know'st thou the land where the lemon-trees bloom, Where the gold orange glows in the deep thicket's gloom . . . ?" (*Wilhelm Meister*, 3.1).

Northeast of the city, in Valverde, an irregular escarpment is made up of lava flows from the complex geology; mineral springs and, sometimes, natural gas springs can be found in the vicinity. The region, inhabited since the second

millennium B.C., boasts various villas, including the Villa Monte d'Oro, which was expanded in the late 1930s by Prince Flavio Borghese of Rome, on his marriage to Princess Manganelli. The original structure, made from lavic ashlar stone, over two and a half feet thick, was only one story high, and the prince had it raised and made more elegant with two side loggias.

On the Viale Regina Margherita, various nineteenth-century dwellings have been inspired by an imaginative eclecticism typical of that flourishing period that enriched the city with significant architecture. The Villa Trigona, buried within a dense garden; the Villa Vecchio and the Villa di Bella, refined through a skillful play of volumes. The Villa Cutore is particularly imposing, and the Villa Modica's garden contains an underground burial chamber, a Roman funerary monument with a circular plan, twenty-three feet (7 m) in diameter.

North of Catania, the town of Acireale was also known as the Viareggio of the south, due to its popularity as an elitist vacation destination, its mild climate, and the substantial wealth and urbanity of its inhabitants. Giosuè Carducci praised it in his *Primavere elleniche*: "Do you know the lovely isle, whose shores / the Ionian sends final fragrant kisses / in whose serene sea lives Galatea and on whose mountains, Acis?" Toward the end of the nineteenth century the Palermitan architect Giuseppe Matricolo built a castle in Acireale for the barons Pennisi di Floristella. The building's style is Gothic-Norman, with numerous mullioned windows and a crenellated coping on the principal facade. A large garden surrounds the elegant dwelling, one of many belonging to this celebrated Sicilian family.

Castello Pennisi di Floristella in Acireale (Catania). The imposing neo-Gothic complex is surrounded by a dense garden of palm trees.

SIRACUSA

In the region of Siracusa, farm complexes were organized around a courtyard, with the main house on one side and service areas and farmers' quarters on the others. These entities were created in the eighteenth century, when the large landed estates were divided up. The result was self-sufficient communities (laic and religious), with granaries, storerooms, threshing rooms, cellars, and mills. The main house, called a *casino* or *casina*,

Right: Torre Milocca in Montalto (Siracusa), fifteenth-century in origin, was built to guard the domain of Acimusa, Milocca, and Pirato.

Below: Villa Italia in Isola (Siracusa).

was always located in a strategic position for supervising the comings and goings of the workers and the basic operations of the estate. There often was also a chapel and a hut for straw, hive-shaped and pierced with holes to facilitate the drying process.

Many houses were built on preexisting structures, such as the farm complex in Tremilia, which encompasses a sixth-century church, or one in San Lorenzo, built around a classical temple, or one in San Marco, built alongside a Byzantine necropolis.

Villa Eleonora di Villadorata in Noto Marina (Siracusa); the long principal facade follows a curved contour typical of the intense Baroque style in the region of Noto.

Lookout towers were renovated and linked to new structures, such as the Lenolina, Milocca, Cubba, or Isola towers, the latter of which is incorporated into the Villa Beneventano del Bosco. Often farm complexes were fortified with walls and crenellations, and moats with drawbridges. The problem of security had an impact not only on building typology but also on local customs. Only by the end of the nineteenth century did they feel safe living in separate farmhouses.

One of the oldest landed estates, in Targia, north of Siracusa, dates back to the thirteenth century. The original castle seems to have been a hunting lodge for Frederick II of Swabia, who enjoyed hunting in the large parks that surrounded his retreats. Only two towers remain from the medieval edifice, and these are now encompassed within the present building, which, with its large corner towers, crenellation, and corbels, takes its inspiration from the earlier structure.

ELEMENTS OF
CONSTRUCTION
AND COMPOSITION

Orders

In Cretan and Minoan architecture the idea of supporting a weight on a wide cushion above a post developed into column capitals, which in turn evolved into the Doric style. The volutes and floral decorations that are progenitors of the Ionic capital were common in the use with the arch. The orders then were revived during the Renaissance, when a rational architectural organization was established. From that time on the orders were used in whatever inventive way the humanists and Mannerists could devise—gigantic, superimposed, rus-

Right: Villa Barbarigo in Noventa (Vicenza).

Pages 264–265: A door knocker in Emilia, with a base depicting a canine head that supports a pair of putti.

ancient architecture of the Near East, while fluted and molded trabeation appeared in Egypt. It was thanks to the cultural climate of Greek civilization that these individual elements were defined in a systematic fashion, in accordance with rules that resulted in harmonious and well-proportioned structures. The Romans further developed the architectural orders codified by the Greeks, combining their tic—and their use spread throughout Europe and the rest of the world. The last period when the architectural orders were rigorously applied resulted from neoclassicism.

Between the seventh and sixth centuries B.C. the Doric and Ionic orders developed individually, representing different branches of a single Hellenic lineage. They emerged in different historical contexts: continenal Greece, invaded by the Dorians, and the Asiatic and island territories, occupied by the Ionians. The Doric order's constituent elements are derived from the wooden construction of their Greek progenitors. The triglyphs seem to represent the memory of the ends of tie beams, while the metopes

derived from the Doric. Since the time of the Greeks the architectural orders have ennobled every "important" style of architecture, conferring stateliness and magnificence even where the designer is lacking in inventiveness.

recall the original axes or clay infill slabs in the attic level. The Romans then added elements to the Hellenistically derived classical orders. The first composite order was derived from the insertion of Ionian volutes into a Corinthian capital, which could already be seen in the Augustan era but became very common after the rediscovery of classical architecture, beginning in the Renaissance. The Tuscan order was

Above: Villa Piovene, Lonedo di Lugo (Vicenza).

Left: A composite capital from L'Encyclopédie by Denis Diderot and Jean Le Rond D'Alembert (1751–66).

Pronaoi

In The Four Books of Architecture *Andrea Palladio translated into drawings his ideas about palaces, villas, and temples. This treatise, published in 1570, echoed work by earlier writers such as Jacopo Vignola and Sebastiano Serlio, which Palladio used as a point of departure to look back at the classical tradition then being rediscovered. Palladio suggested the use of ornate architectural orders for elegant villas and for palaces, while he found the Tuscan order more appropriate for tenant farmers' houses. He gave great attention to the spacing between* columns, *which he closely related to the dimensions of the orders. As a result, the pronaos became a recurring element in stately residential architecture, acquiring increasing grandiosity on the facades of Renaissance villas in Italy and much of Europe.*

The word pronaos *was taken from the Greek, where it indicated the porticoed space in front of the cella of a classical temple. Thus the pronaos was an element associated with religious architecture; only when the form was borrowed by the Romans did it become laicized and*

Villa Ala Ponzone in Sospiro (Cremona).

contribute to the monumental quality of secular buildings.

In the Doric order the diameter of a column at the base was one-fifth of the height, a ratio meant to reflect that between the sole of an athlete's foot and his height. In the Ionic order, the relationship was one-eighth, because reference was to a female body. The volutes of the capital by Michelangelo, who subordinated the framework, dimensions, and spaces between columns to the compositional axes of the facade. When the dimensions were not enlarged, the orders were superimposed, giving rise to double pronaoi, which introduced the principal access to the ground floor, while the upper floor had a balcony.

could bring to mind a woman's braids. And the dense fluting of the shaft the folds in the rich garments of matrons. Designers of merit would develop their own canons to determine the proportions between the pronaos and the body of the building. Some, such as Raphael and Baldassare Peruzzi, linked them to the axes, others to the height of the facade, and still others to the tympanum that crowned the facade and concealed the two pitched sides of the roof. The use of colossal orders also became widespread. These were introduced by Alberti but reworked

Above: Villa Aldini in Bologna.

Left: Villa Spineda in Venegazzù (Treviso).

Tympanums

*T*ympanums (triangular and curved) were widely used as decorative elements above the architrave of doors and windows, particularly as a result of the formal rules of construction developed in the Hellenistic and Roman eras. Generally these are simple closing membranes, without a supporting function, decorated with painting or bas-relief. Their form is not necessarily triangular, and the upper portion can be curved, in which case they are called arched tympanums. These can be depressed arches, acute arches, or a combination, such as those inspired by Islamic art.

After the fourth century architecture moved away from the classical orders, and from the Paleochristian era until the early Middle Ages, door and window openings were at most delimited by a cornice. Architecture at the time

An eclectic tympanum frames the entrance to the Villa Gaslini in Genoa.

of Frederick II saw a return to the classical scheme, flanked by pilaster strips and crowned by trabeation and a triangular pediment. In France this type of portal with concentric arches became a widely disseminated formal device during the Gothic period. The latter era also witnessed a radical transformation of the Romanesque portal. Arches became acute and the exterior archivolt was usually surmounted

by a triangular pediment with spires. In the fifteenth century a return to classicism could be seen not only in the revival of the orders but also in decorative schemes. There was a revival of motifs such as candelabra, grotesques, medallions with heads of Roman emperors, herms, Atlas-type figures, military friezes with shields and armor, festoons, and putti. In the Baroque period compositional schemes became more complicated, with elaborate moldings and broken tympanums. Finally in the nine-

teenth century all the earlier styles, both local and international, were revived, with the addition of new examples imported from China, Egypt, and other exotic locales. These merged with the classical style, resulting in curious hybrids—an amalgam of styles that has formally enriched the villa typology.

Above, left: Villa La Gallina in Florence; right, some variations on the triangular tympanum.

Top: An example of the Baroque broken tympanum from the Villa Loschi Zileri dal Verme in Monteviale (Vicenza).

Acroteria, Spires, and Dovecotes

The term acroterium comes from the Greek akrotérion, which means "highest part." Vitruvius defined these elements as "sculptures placed atop temples," since originally they were used solely for sacred architecture. These ornamental elements were placed at the top and at the side ends of the pediment. In an earlier era the term indicated the base, and only later was the meaning extended to the entire element. The earliest examples were painted terra-cotta disks; later three-dimensional compositions were introduced, using plant shapes, vases, and mythological figures such as the winged Victory. In many cases, the key positions of pronaoi and pediments were marked by obelisks. These were composed of a monolithic shaft of granite or some other hard stone, with the four sides slightly tapered toward the top and covered with inscriptions. Often an obelisk was surmounted by a *spire, sometimes clad in metal to catch the sunlight. Spheres made of stone, marble, terracotta, cement, or—more rarely—metal often crowned the facades of seventeenth- and eighteenth-century villas, interpolated with vases, pinecones, and obelisks. Together with statuary art, urns and vases were the most important vertical elements in the villa's design. One reason these elements were so popular was their adaptability to almost any proportion and decorative motif, without ever losing the symmetry of their circular form. The dovecote motif, in contrast, was a crowning element used above all in "gentlemen's*

houses" in Tuscany, a tradition dating back to Roman times. It was widely used, especially in country dwellings, where it represented an important element in the rural economy and was used for raising edible birds. These winged creatures entered the dovecotes through narrow slit openings. Those who tended the birds

Opposite: Villa Ducale in Colorno (Parma).

Below: A coat of arms on the facade of an ancient villa in the region of Ragusa.

Left: An Este palace in Varese.

entered the dovecote from inside the villa, climbing a steep ladder that led up from the ceiling of the house.

Time Machines

In Other Inquisitions *Jorge Luis Borges wrote: "Time is the substance of which I am made. Time is a river that sweeps me along, but I am the river; it is a tiger that tears me apart, but I am the tiger; it is a fire that consumes me, but I am the fire."* The word for sundial in Italian is meridi-ana, *which is derived from Latin and means "midday"; it is a tool that can function only during daylight hours, with the help of sunlight. The reading of the hour then can be direct (the num-ber indicated corresponds to the hour at that moment) or indirect—for example, the hours remaining until sunset can be indicated, or those that have passed since dawn. Over the centuries many different types of sundials have been devel-oped, with different types of readings. From the Roman Empire up to and including the thir-teenth century, time was measured from dawn to dusk, dividing the day into twelve hours that expanded and contracted seasonally. Later the*

Above: Villa Mapelli in Ponte San Pietro (Bergamo).

Right: Villa Carlotta in Tremezo (Como).

sundial with Babylonian hours was used widely; in this case the twenty-four hours had a constant duration and began with sunrise (as they did in Babylonia). Midday coincided with the high point of the sun on the local meridian. With the dissemination of Arab culture throughout the Mediterranean basin, people began to measure time beginning from sunset, which was the custom in the East. Sundials with Italic hours were used in Italy until the mid-nineteenth century

In the last century France exported the sundial with French hours (also known as modern, astronomical, or European hours) to the Piedmont and the rest of Italy. This type became the most widely used, in part because it was the easiest to read. The twenty-four hours had a constant duration and began counting from midnight.

To embellish and beautify these tools, various types of artisans spent a great deal of time inserting phrases or mottos, sometimes cryptic, sometimes explicit. These phrases, which frequently contained genuine and ancient wisdom, addressed the theme of the imperturbable passage of time and death, which inexorably drew near. They were accompanied by drawings of floral and astral elements, such as the sun, moon, and stars, and the signs of the zodiac. The frames were quite imaginative and varied in style. Clocks also were extremely popular with both patrons and designers. The first evidence of clocks applied to towers and facades dates to the thirteenth century. From the Renaissance on, placing a clock on the facade of one's residence implied that one controlled the course of events.

Time and its different forms have long punctuated the rhythms of villa life. On tympanums and pediments, in simple frames or amid voluptuous stuccowork, tools for measuring time distinguish a facade. Now as then, these instruments remind us to "seize the day," since we never know what tomorrow will bring.

Above: Isola Madre in Stresa (Novara).

Below: Villa Pegazzera in Montalto (Pavia).

Attics

Originally the term attic *indicated a low masonry coping element, located above the cornice of the facade, with the function of hiding the roof. Depending on the historical period, the attic was variously decorated with balustrades, statues, vases, moldings, fascias, and whatever else might lighten the composition.*

took on a merely decorative value, as did pinecones, which were characteristic of all classical and then Renaissance architecture. Spheres were also very common. Attics sometimes included coats of arms, shields, clocks, or trophies. The latter were originally symbols of victory, and the ancient Greeks used to arrange

The simplest examples, composed of an openwork screen, perhaps decorated with rosettes or bas-reliefs, could be completed with urns, pinecones, spheres, vases, and obelisks. The urn originally signified death but soon

the conquered enemy's armor on tree trunks.

A widespread decorative element for the attic was the Greek key or maze design. This was made up of a sequence of alternating straight lines and right angles. The result was a symmetrical, interwoven form; the background motif could be reversed, placed next to a mirror image, or rotated. Other motifs could be inserted into the lines that made up the design. These might be curving lines, sometimes brought out by simple chromatic contrast. The wave motif, also known as a Greek,

the arabesque; it was derived from various examples discovered in the interiors of Roman dwellings. Knot motifs and various other interlaced elements formed two bands, densely interwoven or occasionally wound around a row of disks. The bands could be wrapped, one upon another; in other cases, the disks are transformed

Vitruvian, or continuous curl volute, is a curvilinear version of the geometric Greek key design. In certain instances the motif was supplemented with central rosettes and foliage.

Another decorative element for the attic was

into diamond shapes. A rosette often occupied the central space. Like other decorative motifs, the attic crowns the villa, giving it a stately and "important" appearance; it rarely fulfilled a practical function.

Above: A long balustrade conceals the roof, ennobling this facade.

Roofs and Domes

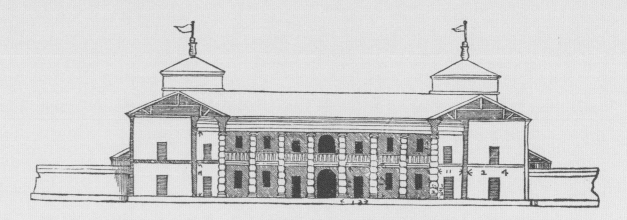

The most common type of roof is a two-sided, pitched saddle roof, while a four-sided roof is known as a pavilion roof. There also are single-pitched shed roofs. The slope varies and is steeper in northern regions, to shed winter snow. In these cases, mansards are inserted either in the spaces between the ceiling of the last floor and the roof, or in habitable areas that face the outside, through the inclusion of dormer win-dows and covered roof terraces. These can have continuous eaves or ridges, depending on which level they are built.

In Italian the word for roof is tetto, derived from the Latin tectum, which means "covered." Cupola, or dome, also derives from Latin and means "barrel." It specifies a curvilinear, more or less regular roofing element that covers a circular, square, or polygonal space. The dome has a double meaning: seen from outside, it is a

Above and opposite: Drawings of a villa from Andrea Palladio's Four Books of Architecture.

Below: Vincenzo Scamozzi's Villa Pisani in Lonigo (Vicenza).

reproduction of the terrestrial globe; from the inside, it is a miniature of the celestial vault. Celestial and human dimensions enter into dialogue once again through architecture, a faithful mirror of man's terrestrial and ideal ambitions and aspirations.

In the Renaissance, when architectural dimensions increased, the double spherical vault was introduced, with an air space on the inside). One vault supported the lining of the roof, the other the interior decoration. This period also saw the introduction of spherical domes, with longitudinal ribbing. In the Baroque era the elliptical dome was widely employed, as seen in the work of Francesco Borromini.

Depending on its form, a dome could be spherical, hemispherical, depressed, raised, pointed, globular, pendentive, vaulted, or segmented. When the space to be covered is not square, a connecting element is introduced in the form of a drum between the dome and the impost.

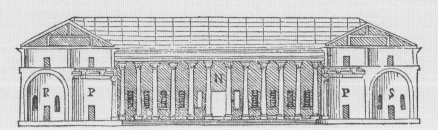

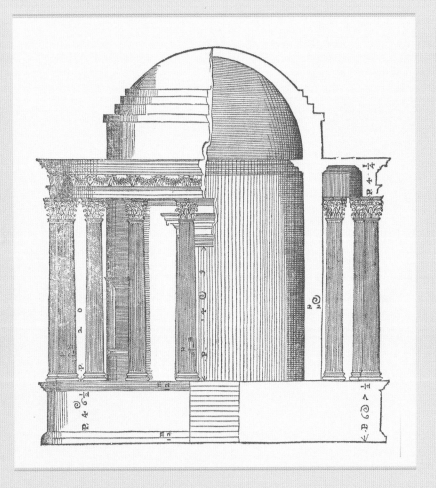

Doors and Portals

Below: Villa Garzoni in Pontecasale (Padua).

Below right: Medici villa in Artimino (Florence).

In all cultures, the entrance to the dwelling whenever possible has been located at the center of the facade, a position that confers importance. But such a central location is not always possible, due to a preexisting condition or for other functional reasons. In such cases the most common solution is to locate the entrance to one side of the facade, possibly with an analogous structure (whether true or faux) at the opposite end, to act as a pendant and reestablish the building's symmetry.

Doors can be divided into three categories,

be covered, without the need for intermediary supports. In this case, however, the voussoirs that make up the arch are subject to compression and bear down upon the springers with lateral thrust. Finally there are arch systems inserted into a rectangular space, where the archivolt is superimposed by an encompassing architrave that absorbs the thrust of the arch, which thus can be freely decorated and embellished.

In Italy the most common type of door is based on the trilith system, and the space that it defines can be rectangular or slightly trape-

depending on the structural system to which they belong. The most common is the trilith, where the architrave rests its weight on side piers, known as springers, eliminating any lateral thrust. Arched doors allow greater spans to

zoidal. Sometimes the architrave-pier system has three-dimensional decoration and projects out from the edge of the wall. Other systems are decorated with fluting that recalls earlier wooden elements.

Where doors and main entrances cannot be emphatically delineated, a passage may be defined through a portal. According to modern usage, a portal is a monumental entrance to a building complex. It can be either the passage that leads to the dwelling itself or, more often, the element that leads to the complex's other

Corte Cappelletta, Palidano (Mantua).

Far left: Villa Levrano d'Aquino in Taranto.

Left: Villa Terzi in Trescore Balneario (Bergamo).

components, such as the garden, courtyard, and so on. The portal links the public road to the architectural structure that makes up the dwelling or any other sort of building, including those set aside for other use. The portal can be classified with doors and entranceways. At times it is more stately and important, marked by grandiose architectural and decorative language.

Door Knockers

Above: An elegant door knocker in wrought iron.

Below: A simple door knocker for gaining entry at the service door of the Castello Uzzano.

Door knockers fashioned in the shape of a ring or also a palinette were very widespread even during classical antiquity. In both Greece and the territories of imperial Rome, plates have been found with circles connected to masks in the form of lions, medusas, and other mythological figures. These early classical examples were revived and embellished in the humanist period by skilled artisans, who engraved and embossed iron and bronze. In Italy these artisans were active for the most part in the cities of Padua, Venice, and Florence. The simple ring thus evolved into different forms (heart, lyre, serpent), embellished with diamond-point, shell, and medallion shapes. In the Renaissance many noble families had their coats of arms reproduced, along with new

Background drawing:
A sixteenth-century
door knocker.

Below: A finely worked
seventeenth-century
door knocker.

figurative elements such as fauns, satyrs, drag-
ons, sea gods, and whatever else the fervid
humanist and then Mannerist imagination
could invent. Their presence, while detached
form the original function, bears effective witness to a period when the rhythms of life were
slower and, perhaps, more humane.

Door knockers were created in pairs, with the
one attached to the right-hand door (which
was opened first) serving as the actual sounding device. The left-hand knocker had a purely
decorative function. This typology was widely
taken up for wall rings used for tying up
horses, or for supporting torches or flags. The
variety of uses to which these rings were put
ensured their success, and so artisans indulged
their imaginations in ever-stranger forms.

The door knocker could be made of iron,
bronze, cast iron, or brass. Its hammering on
the wooden door, amplified by the atrium that
acted as a sounding box, once announced visitors to the masters of the house, but its characteristic sound has become increasingly rare.

Windows and Balconies

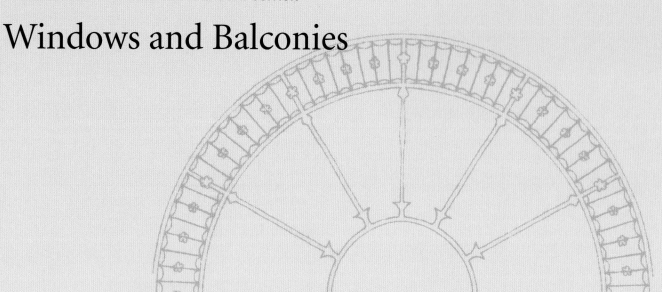

*T*he evolution of the window is tied to the materials and static construction systems used in different periods and regions. This is a story of inventions, customs, official functions, and the need for privacy and security. The window developed from the earliest openings in nomads' tents (barely screened off by interwoven strips of leather) to arrow slits, to architraved windows, to the first two- and three-mullioned windows. Gothic architecture was characterized by a rhythmic arrangements of windows, differing from floor to floor, depending on the lighting needs of the interior spaces and resulting in unusual harmonies on the facades. Renaissance window schemes, characterized by vertical axes and rigorous symmetry, were composed like architectural orders, with pilaster strips, columns, tympanums, and trabeations. The proportions and rhythm of the facades were meant to have precise relationships to the har-

Above: Fan-shaped lunette, eighteenth century.

Right: Villa Bonocore in Palermo.

monic laws that governed the entire universe. Finally there is the window with the outward-curving grating, its sill supported by airy volutes on axis with the jambs.

Well known models are the Palladian window, its broad semicircle divided into three sections, and the tripartite Venetian window, which, with its airy openings, is more a loggia than a window.

A window open all the way to the floor, with an overhang, even minimal, jutting out from the facade, or supported by corbels and protected by a railing, parapet, or balustrade, is called a balcony. On a much smaller scale, it is called a pioggiolo—"little terrace" in Italian. When a balcony embraces an entire facade it becomes a gallery. Balconies might be placed above the main entrance door, or sometimes expanded to include two or more windows; a gallery, as well as extending along the entire facade, might even turn the corners.

In the fifteenth and sixteenth centuries balconies often rested upon a skirting projecting out from the plane of the facade, or above the cornice string course, or on columns with trabeation. During this same period the corbels supporting the balustrades were given refined and virtuosic decorative treatment that embellished the balconies, becoming a fundamental motif on the facade. This tendency was accentu-

ated considerably in the Baroque period, when balconies were transformed into veritable jewels of ornamental sculpture. At first the structure supporting the overhang was made from wood; two beams were set into the masonry, upon which the shelf of the base, made from wooden planks, rested. From the Middle Ages on it was common to use small supporting corbels with cornices of one or more courses, especially for shallow balconies. Moreover many balconies used marble slabs for their bases, or stone supported by corbels. Balconies could also rest on columns or vaults; depending on the complexity of the workmanship, these might form a sort of pronaos leading to the main entrance.

Above left: Villa Visconti Citterio in Brignano (Bergamo).

Above right: Villa Terzi in Trescore (Bergamo).

Towers and Turrets

The expression of power always has been one of the functions of architecture. This function is not easy to isolate, recurring as it does in buildings of every type. Undoubtedly, however, it is vertical elements that most obviously attempt to express power and wealth. Through these constructions every civilization proclaims its power and glory in forms that survive its existence and

at the corners of the main facade, although there are many more examples of small central towers, a typology that developed chiefly from the fifteenth to the eighteenth century. These were accessible small towers or turrets, often surrounded by balconies or at least windows, sometimes covered. Corner turrets, on the other hand, might project out from the plane of the facade and clearly were derived from the corner towers of medieval castles. Initially thick and massive, the latter evolved into more graceful and slender forms until, in some cases, they closely resembled spires. Both corner and centrally located towers were sometimes equipped with clocks, sundials, coats of arms, and inscriptions.

Above, left: Villa Corsi in Sesto Fiorentino (Florence).

Above, right: Castello, Ghignolo Po (Pavia).

Background drawing: Turret from a Strozzi farm complex, in the Roman campagna (fifteenth century).

Opposite: Castello Tafuri in Portopalo (Siracusa).

decline. In fact, the more confident and long-sighted a culture, the more its architecture tends to rise skyward. In earlier times, towers served to survey the territory, to sight the enemy in time. Then they were used as fortified residences—the renowned tower-houses so widely disseminated in post-medieval Italy. The height of the tower, which once was meant to frighten attackers, now expressed the owner's power and prestige. In villas, towers preferably were placed at the center or

Man has always built towers; the aspiration to height answers a desire to expand one's horizons and to break beyond the confines of one's surroundings. Indeed, these ephemeral forms have long represented man's illusion that he might extend his reach infinitely, even reaching the sky. The higher man built his towers, the more acute his delusion. But spirituality, as well as power, has always been linked to the concept of height; after all, paradise lies in the heavens.

Watchtowers

In villa architecture the watchtower, an element of castle typology, maintained its defensive character, including slit windows to be used in the event of conflict. As sieges became unlikely, the watchtower evolved into a protected location for observing the outbuildings surrounding the main house. Generally the watchtower was accessible from the second floor (piano nobile), often from the master

offer many occasions for decoration. The supporting base often consisted of superimposed concentric circles, or else a conical shape in stone, or projecting beams.

The most common roof form for the watchtower was a round dome or a sloping roof, often topped by a sphere. In certain examples the body of the watchtower continued down to the ground as a bastion, giving the villa a

Villa Guardatoia in Pescia (Lucca).

Right: Palazzo Pellicciari, a farm complex in Gravina (Bari).

bedroom, or from some room located at a corner, which offered the best views from the villa. The word in Italian for watchtower, garitta, is derived from the Provençal garida ("defense," "protection"), and originally indicated a minuscule structure for sheltering a sentry, located along the walkway or at the entrance to military buildings.

The watchtower's dimensions are always quite modest, as it was meant to accommodate a single sentry. It is covered, to provide shelter for a prolonged stay. The spartan form did not

fortified appearance.

In practice these structures served as a defense against incursions by pirates (when the dwelling was situated on the coast) or the bands of outlaws that infested the countryside in the nineteenth century. In fact it was during this period that the watchtower was most widely disseminated in residential architecture; earlier it had been chiefly an addition to castles and fortresses. Throughout northern Italy fortified farm complexes guarded olive groves, vineyards, and almond plantations.

Heraldry

*T*he shield, being the main component of a knight's armor, is the most common shape for the coat of arms. In general this is divided into parts, vertically, horizontally, or diagonally, resulting in various shapes: divided, truncated, cut, and so on. The ornamentation placed above or around the coat of arms varies. There might be a helmet above, which in the case of prelates is replaced by a pope's tiara or cardinal's cap. Depending on rank, a crown might also surmount the composition, sometimes made out of iron for greater plastic effect. Other embellishments are made from fabric, ropes with tassels, scrolls, or plant or animal elements. Beginning in the sixteenth century the incorporation of family mottos became popular. The elaborate graphic search for new symbols continued until the French Revolution, when heraldry suffered a harsh blow, since it was identified with

tyranny. Sculpted in stone, marble, and occasionally in iron, coats of arms, in most and particularly in the most ancient cases, were executed in bas-relief and superimposed on the masonry structure. Sometimes, in more modest cases, they were carved from the same material as the structure and thus permanent for all purposes. From the Renaissance on they were also made in three dimensions, with many concave and convex features, and the addition of color increased legibility and created new spatial hierarchies. They usually were attached to the supporting masonry structure with iron brackets and placed on the coping of facades and balustrades, frequently inserted into pediments or on the keystones of entrance archways and portals. Less frequently they were positioned in a corner, a solution adopted more for city palaces than for villas.

Today the coats of arms of patrician families still decorate family homes and outbuildings, indelible marks of ownership. Evidence of a stately past, they exhibit the history of a residence, narrate changes in ownership, provide a decorative touch, and for a chosen few, take the place of a visiting card.

Beyond its historical meanings, the coat of arms also serves as an elegant decorative motif.

Above: Coat of arms on the facade of the Villa Palagonia, Bagheria (Palermo), and the coat of arms above the entrance to the Medici villa La Petraia in Florence.

Left: Coat of arms of the Villa Guardatoia in Pescia (Pistoia).

Opposite, top: Coat of arms on the Villa Mercadante in Palermo; opposite, bottom, the Orsini coat of arms in Bomarzo (Viterbo).

Mosaics and Sponge Stone

Mosaics, shells, and cobblestone paving are only some of the many ways of decorating and embellishing bare masonry. These are not precious materials, but they give precious and refined effects, proof that appearances are always more important than reality where "illusion" can become art. The Romans put these devices to extensive use. In the East during the Middle Ages a particular type of mosaic, made

The Mannerists began to use this decorative technique in conjunction with villa architecture. Mosaics were employed in the decoration of architectural structures annexed to the main house, such as grottoes, nymphaea, exedrae, staircases, niches, and fountains. These are the so-called rustic mosaics, heirs to classical decorations, and they also include imitations of rocks, achieved through casting using a porous

Above, background image: Pebble mosaic from the Palazzo Giugni in Florence.

Right: Nymphaeum, Villa Aldobrandini in Frascati (Rome).

up of marble and stone tiles, was common. Valued in Byzantine times, this technique became extremely popular in Islamic art for the decoration of floors and interior walls. The tiles are of various sizes, generally triangular, star-shaped, or rectangular, and the colors range from yellow to red, in combinations with white and black.

material, called sponge stone. The material employed for this casting technique is mortar, poured into various layers using different tones of the same color. Pebbles were used in early mosaic work, but later semiprecious stones, marbles, shells, pieces of glass, terra-cotta, mother-of-pearl, and enamels were preferred.

Mosaic is an ancient art, and over time the technique has changed very little. The process recalls the preparation of wall surfaces for frescoes. An initial layer of rough plaster must be applied, then a second smooth layer, upon which the drawing is made, and finally a last, thin layer, which becomes the bed for the tiles. It is a time-consuming operation, but the results are often surprising.

Left: Nymphaeum, Villa d'Este in Cernobbio (Como).

Below, left: Fountain from the Royal Hall of the Villa Farnese in Caprarola (Viterbo); below, right, nymphaeum, Palazzo Budini Gattai in Florence.

Drawing Rooms and Galleries

The word salon, *meaning "drawing room," is derived from the Lombard term* sala, *used for a building consisting of a single room. The word gradually evolved and came to define the principal space of a house, around which the other rooms are laid out. The typologies are as varied as the uses to which such rooms are put. There are arms rooms (for bayonet training), game rooms (with billiards and other table games), music rooms (for private concerts), and of course ballrooms.*

Above: Architecture, sallon. Vue perspective sur la longeur, *engraving from* L'Encyclopédie *by Diderot and D'Alembert (1751–1766).*

Opposite: Drawing room in the Villa Borghese in Rome.

In classical Greece the places of honor for the master of the house and the most highly regarded guests were located at the two ends of the table. The Romans considered placement at the central triclinium to be a sign of privilege, and both central and side triclinia were located at the center of a large room. The use of the drawing room as a dining room continued into the Middle Ages, when benches were set up with long rectangular tables, well suited to halls of the same shape.

Galleries are similar to drawing rooms, but they have a different purpose. The first examples are rectangular rooms in sixteenth-century French castles, full of stuccowork, paintings, and other works of art. Later the use of mirrors became widespread, which helped to dematerialize the walls and make rooms more airy. The most famous gallery of mirrors is undoubtedly the seventeenth-century Galerie des Glaces *in the royal palace of Versailles. The use of mirrors was then revived to amplify rococo spaces with illusionistic effects. One or two stories high, drawing rooms and galleries were accessible from the outside or reached through a vestibule. They provided places of assembly for social rituals, which, enlarged, celebrated the patron's status. An equivalent is found in every culture and tradition, although with the passage of time, the relationships and dimensions have changed.*

Places set aside for receptions, drawing rooms and galleries often provided settings for sumptuous balls. Before serving as ballrooms, drawing rooms had accommodated private theater performances, which in the fifteenth and sixteenth centuries moved between courtyards and interiors, specially equipped with semicircular steps and sumptuous decorations.

Oratories

The word oratory *comes from the Latin* oratorium, *a "place for prayer," and was used to indicate a place of worship, either isolated or within a villa, set aside for a small group of the faithful. The word* chapel, *derived from the Latin* sacellum, *originally referred to a portion of the cloak of Saint Martin of Tours, preserved in a small room located in the Merovingian royal palace that became a place of prayer and veneration. In the case of the villa, both words are used for a space where mass may be celebrated, subject to authorization from church authorities. Access is restricted, and services can be private (reserved for the master of the house), semipublic (open to people from outside under specific conditions), or public (anyone is admitted). When space allowed, private patrons installed a women's gallery and box seats from which they could participate in public religious functions, without mixing with the general public. These private galleries, placed above the public area or to the sides of the altar, were entered directly from the main house. Often a wooden grille isolated the lords and ladies of the house from view.*

Oratories generally consist of a single space, vaulted or with exposed beams. Sometimes the nave and presbytery are partitioned off from an adjacent sacristy. The facade usually has a triangular or curvilinear pediment that hides the pitched roof. There often are two entrances, one private, from the villa, and another on the principal facade of the chapel. The campanile, either a tower or a bell gable, rises from the roof. Having a chapel in one's home always has served to show support for religion and ally oneself with the clergy. When these spaces were open to the public, the masters of the house also could take control of the spiritual activities of those under their protection.

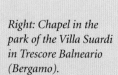

Right: Chapel in the park of the Villa Suardi in Trescore Balneario (Bergamo).

Opposite: Chapel facing the interior courtyard of the Villa Conchia in Monopoli (Bari).

APPENDICES

Glossary

Abacus: Stone slab placed above a capital; its form varies, depending on the architectural order.

acanthus: Plant native to the Mediterranean basin, with bold, architectural leaves that are used as a motif on Corinthian capitals.

acroterium: Decorative element placed at the summit or corners of a fronton. In some cases the word indicates only the base that supports the ornamentation.

aedicule: Small architectural element designed to shelter sacred images, which became a decorative element in Roman gardens.

amphora: A large vessel with two handles, generally long in shape with a narrow mouth; in classical antiquity it was used to transport liquids, and it has since been used as an ornamental garden feature. The name is derived from the Greek *amphoreus*, "object with two handles."

antefix: Vertical decoration that once had a load-bearing function, located on the edge of a roof.

antemium: Stylized plant motif.

arabesque: Decoration with elaborate, stylized, and repetitive geometrical or floral motifs, introduced by the Arabs.

architrave: The main beam of the trabeation, the upper element enclosing doors and windows.

archivolt: The upper face of an arch, on doors and windows; the decoration contained in a band that follows the curvature of the arch.

ashlar: A squared-off block of stone, more or less finely worked, used in masonry construction, often with a decorative function.

Atlas: Very large male figure supporting a trabeation, taking the place of a column or pillar.

auditorium: Area set aside for the audience in a theater, indoors or in the landscape.

aviary: Small structure in which birds are kept.

Baglio: Residential-agricultural complex in southern Italy, with both a main house and structures used for agricultural activities and crop storage.

baluster: Small pier or column, which can have various shapes.

balustrade: Parapet formed by a series of small columns with shaped shafts, atop a continuous base and surmounted by a continuous molding; also, a series of balusters.

barchessa: A Venetian term for a farmhouse. Initially it referred to buildings designed for agricultural use, but later it also indicated guest quarters located next to the main house.

basin: A low container for water with its edges turned down, generally made of terra-cotta or metal. A furnishing element needed for irrigation, usually mixing utility and pleasure. In the Arab world it became a source of cooling and a place for aquatic games; in the Christian world it is mostly used as a decorative and compositional element in gardens.

belvedere: An elevated area with architectural elements for moments of leisure, such as pavilions, terraces, and turrets.

boss: A squared-off block of stone.

boxwood: Evergreen shrub of the Buxacaea family with small oval, shiny leaves, used for hedges and topiary art.

broderie: A flower bed typical of seventeenth- and eighteenth-century formal gardens, especially in France, "embroidered" with complex designs achieved with flowers, evergreens, and gravel.

bucranium: Decorative motif in classical art, depicting an ox head between two festoons.

Capital: Decorated block placed between the top of the column and the architrave or impost of the arch that the column supports.

cartouche: Decorative element, in marble or stone, sculpted in the form of a scrolled parchment, with an inscription or coat of arms inside.

caryatid: Female figure that replaces a column or pier.

casena: Small farmhouse located in the region of Palermo.

casino: A lodge; an intimate and private place, set in a natural or artificial "wild area," in contrast to official court locations.

casino di caccia: A hunting lodge, used for rest and recreation during expeditions; not equipped with bedrooms.

cherub: Painted or sculpted portrayal of an angel in Christian religious art.

cippus: Funerary marker made from a broken-off column or pier.

cistern: Masonry structure, usually below ground level, where rainwater is collected.

coat of arms: Noble coat of arms or aristocratic insignia in the form of a shield.

coffer: Lacunar decoration of a flat or curved ceiling.

corbel: Overhanging, load-bearing element; small arch supporting the course of merlons and embrasures.

cordonata: Flight of steps or a narrow stepped street, placed diagonally to a central staircase, forming a perspectival axis.

cornice: Upper terminal band of a facade, placed below the gutter line; also the decorative band that outlines a doorway.

cryptoporticus: A ground-level portico, in villas in imperial Rome, open on one side, with arches linking the house to the garden.

Dado: Main component of a column pedestal.

dentil: Tooth-shaped element in a cornice.

dormer: Room set into the roof, illuminated by windows of various kinds.

dovecote: Turret superimposed upon rural structures, meant for raising small groups of pigeons.

drops: Small, cylindrical decorative elements originally used only in the Doric order.

Echinus: A convex molding component, shaped like a halved egg.

echinus: Overhanging element beneath the abacus of a column capital.

embrasure: The gap between the corbels supporting merlons, used to drop objects onto besieging forces.

entasis: The swelling in section of a column shaft.

espalier: Method of training and pruning tree branches so that they extend at set angles, at regular levels. The term also refers to a wall or "fence" created with a row of interlocking trees trained in this manner.

exedra: From a Greek word meaning "outside seat," a colonnaded or porticoed semicircle, placed at the end of sacred and secular spaces and outdoor spaces.

Fastigium: Apex of the central part of an architectural structure, generally made with volutes, and featuring coats of arms, clocks, and other decorative elements.

festoon: Bas-relief or painted decoration in the form of a draped garland of branches ornamented with flowers and putti.

fishpond: Basin for raising edible fish. It can be a purely utilitarian element, or it can assume elaborate and decorative forms.

fistula: Ancient water pipe made from lead, used for supplying fountains and spigots.

flat arch: Depressed arch used in place of the architrave to enclose the upper part of doors and small windows.

fluting: Vertical concavities that run along the shaft of a column.

frieze: Horizontal decorative band at the center of the trabeation, in varying styles, depending on the architectural order.

Garland: Botanical ornamentation, sometimes made of stone or stucco, used as an architectural decoration. Different plants used in garlands have specific connotations (the oak indicates power, the laurel fame, and so on).

gazebo: From the English *to gaze*, this is a sort of covered belvedere.

grotesque: Decoration inspired by arabesques with sphinxes, leaves, branches, and animals, executed in fresco or stucco.

grotto: Natural or artificial cavelike space or ravine used as a shelter from the summer heat; has an implication of a vague sense of mystery. In some cases grottoes are hidden by waterworks.

guilloche: An ornamental pattern composed of interwoven ribbons, used to embellish moldings.

Herb garden: A space in a Renaissance garden dedicated to medicinal herbs and those herbs needed for cooking and making perfume.

herm: Sculpture on a pier, depicting a human head and part of the bust, with both decorative and static functions.

hermitage: Isolated and solitary area, usually walled, used for meditation, located in grottoes or nymphaea

hortus conclusus: A small medieval walled garden, organized into simple flower beds.

Impost: Block on which an arch rests, usually overhanging.

impost plane: Supporting plane for arches and domes.

Lantern: A superstructure on a roof or dome, generally in the form of a circular or polygonal turret, used to bring light into the space below.

lemon house: Greenhouse where lemon trees are kept in pots during the cold months.

lunette: A window above a door.

Mask: A decorative element consisting of a face distorted to appear like a monster.

masseria: Farm estate evolved from coastal towers (see p. 185), name for villa in Puglia.

maze: A pattern of tall hedges arranged in a composition, rectilinear or curved, meant to disorient visitors.

merlon: Toothlike (square or swallow-tailed) crenellation at the top of the perimeter walls in fortified structures, which serves to protect soldiers on watch. Sometimes merlons are used as a decorative element to crown the walls enclosing a garden.

metope: The space between triglyphs in a Doric frieze.

molding: A continuous decorative element, smooth or with repeated motifs.

motulus: Decorative element typical of classical trabeations, jutting out under the cornice.

Nymphaeum: A place originally meant for nymphs; by extension any construction with grottoes and fountains.

Occhio: Round or oval window (*occhio* means "eye") used especially in the Baroque and Rococo periods.

oculus: Circular opening in the center of a dome.

orangery: A greenhouse where orange trees are kept in pots during the cold months of the year.

orchard: In the mid-eighteenth century this term was used to describe a section of a stately garden reserved for the cultivation of fruit trees, which were arrayed in a rigid geometric scheme.

order: A harmonized composition of columns, capitals, trabeation, and pediment developed in Greek architecture and revived in the Humanist era. The Classical orders are Doric, Ionic, and Corinthian; later the colossal and rustic orders were added.

orto, orti: A rural property with farmers' dwellings and, sometimes, places for the visiting landowner to stay.

Parastas: A pier slightly projecting from the wall line, similar to a pilaster slip but with static functions.

park: A large wooded area, full of game and used for hunting, including with nets.

parterre: A flat, treeless space with low hedges that form geometric compartments or refined scrolled patterns. Generally it is intersected by paths that subdivide it into flowerbeds.

pavilion: A structure isolated in a garden or park, functioning as a belvedere and rest area for walkers.

pediment: Triangular space contained between a trabeation and the slopes of a roof, typical of classical architecture.

pendentive: Linking element between a dome or a polygonal roof and the underlying supporting structure, which is either square or in any case with fewer sides than the roof.

pergola: Walkway covered with wooden beams or other cross supports, which supports climbing plants.

peristyle: From the Greek, meaning "surrounding colonnade," a portico that surrounds a courtyard.

pilaster strip: A projecting element on a wall, originally without base or capital, having an essentially decorative function.

pronaos: Portico composed of columns and a tympanum projecting from the plane of the facade.

propylaeum: Entrance to monumental buildings with several doorways.

protome: Decorative element in ancient art depicting a human or animal head in relief.

pulvinar: Convex, projecting frieze used as decoration.

putto: Statue depicting a young boy, usually nude, often used as a decorative element in fountains.

Ribbing: Line of intersection between two vaults.

rocaille: Decoration comprising rocks, shells, and artificial stalactites, especially employed in grottos at the end of the sixteenth century. The term later came to refer to period in the Rococo style.

rosette: Round decorative element with a stylized flower at the center.

rustication: Facing of exterior walls made with ashlars, squared and worked stones.

Selvatico: Miniature forest set aside for hunting

Serlian window: Window with a large central aperture, generally arched, and two smaller side apertures, often surmounted by an eye. Published for the first time by Sebastiano Serlio, it was extensively used by Andrea Palladio.

span: The distance between the centers of two columns in a colonnade.

sponge stone: Artificial facing that imitates rocky walls, stalactites, and stalagmites; used as decoration in grottoes and nymphaea.

string course: A decorative horizontal band on the facade that corresponds to the demarcation between one floor and another.

Tambour: Cylinder linking a dome and the supporting masonry, generally used in roofing for drawing rooms and chapels.

telamon: Pier made up of male figures.

theater of greenery: A space for open-air performances, created from pruned shrubs and trees.

Cypress and laurel often are used, and the seating is made from appropriately trimmed boxwood. Usually it is embellished with statues. If waterworks are included, the space is called a "water theater."

tholos: Small round pavilion at the center of a basin or pool, which in Roman times served as an aviary.

topiary: A technique of training or pruning shrubs or trees into preestablished forms.

torus: Convex molding at the base of a column.

trabeation: Compound element made up of the architrave, frieze, and cornice, resting on the columns in classical architectural orders.

trellis: A structure woven from reeds, wicker, twigs, and other wooden elements, used as infill, repairs, or support.

triglyph: Part of a frieze in the Doric order, alternating with the metope.

trompe-l'oeil: From the French, meaning "deceive the eye," wall painting that simulates architecture or landscape views, expanding the space in illusionistic fashion.

trullo: A dwelling of the Apulia region of Italy, roofed with conical constructions of corbeled dry masonry.

truss: Small corbel in Corinthian or composite orders.

tympanum: Triangular or semicircular space enclosed by the cornice of a pediment.

Urn: Ancient vase used for cremation ashes, included in Romantic parks as archaeological relics.

Vaulting cell: Each of the parts into which a vault is divided.

velata: An artificial waterfall, which creates a mist so subtle and wide it resembles a veil.

veranda: A space in a house that extends toward the outdoors and has large windows, in some cases glassed in.

vestibule: Antechamber or entrance to a drawing room.

vigna: In addition to the common meaning, "vineyard," in the region of Latium until the nineteenth century this referred to a stately suburban or extra-urban residence endowed with large, planned green spaces.

viridarium: Portion of a garden reserved for evergreen trees.

volute: Compositional element characterized by spiral lines.

Water chain: Succession of small cups and cascades that create a path, generally rectilinear, for descending water.

winter garden: A large, habitable greenhouse used as a winter garden in northern Europe. The various species, which cannot tolerate the winter climate, are kept in pots and arranged in elegant compositions.

BIBLIOGRAPHY

Abruzzo dei castelli. Aquila: Carsa, *1988.*

Ackerman, J. S. *La villa: Forma e ideologia.* Turin: Edizioni di Comunità, 2000.

Acton, H. *Ville toscane.* Milan: Mondadori, 1973.

Adami, G., M. Foschi, and S. Venturi. *Ville dell'Emilia romagna: Dai fasti del Settecento al villino urbano.* Milan: Silvana Editoriale, 1982.

Alidori, L. *Le dimore dei Medici in Toscana.* Florence: Polistampa, 1995.

Alpago Novello, A. *Ville della provincia di Belluno.* Milan: Rusconi, 1982.

Amadei, G. *Signorie padane dei Gonzaga.* Mantua: Publi Paolini, 1982.

Andreini Galli, N. *Ville pistoiesi.* Pistoia: Cassa di Risparmio di Pistoia e Pescia, 1989.

Avagnina, M. Tiepolo: *Le ville vicentine.* Milan: Electa, 1990.

Azzi Visentini, M. *La villa in Italia: Quattrocento e Cinquecento.* Milan: Electa, 1995.

Bagatti Valsecchi, P. F., A. M. Cito Filomarino, and F. Süss. *Ville della Brianza.* Vol. 1. Milan: Rusconi, 1980.

Bajard, S., and R. Bencini. *Villas and Gardens of Tuscany.* Paris: Terrail, 1993.

Bartolotti, E., E. Colle, and M. Guarraccino. *Napoleone all'Elba: Le residenze.* Livorno: Sillabe, 1997.

Basehart, J. *Italia meravigliosa: Palazzi, castelli, ville.* Milan: Rizzoli, 1990.

Bassi, E. *Ville della provincia di Venezia.* Milan: Rusconi, 1988.

Battiloti, D. *Le ville del Palladio.* Milan: Electa, 1990.

Belli Barsali, I. *Ville del Lazio.* Novara: De Agostini, 1983.

———. *Ville di Roma.* Milan: Rusconi, 1983.

———. *Ville e committenti dello Stato di Lucca.* Lucca: Maria Pacini Fazzi, 1980.

———. *Ville e giardini del Capannorese.* Lucca: Maria Pacini Fazzi, 1987.

Belli Barsali, I., and M. G. Branchetti. *Ville della campagna romana.* Milan: Rusconi, 1981.

Bertoni, E. *Villa faentine.* Bologna: Bologna University Press, n.d.

Bodefeld, G. *Ville venete.* Milan: Idealibri, 1990.

Bosi, E. *Di castello in castello: Il Chianti.* Milan: Il Bargello, 1990.

———. *Di castello in castello: Il Chianti.* Milan: Trainer International, 1990.

———. *Di castello in castello: Il Senese.* Milan: Trainer International, 1990.

Bové, V. *Veneto Villas.* Venice: Arsenale, 1998.

Canova, A. *Di villa in villa.* Treviso: Canova, 1990.

———. *Le ville della provincia di Belluno.* Treviso: Canova, 1994.

———. *Le ville della provincia di Rovigo: Itinerari.* Treviso: Canova, 1993.

Cantone, G., and I. Prozzillo. *Case di Capri: Ville, palazzi, grandi dimore.* Naples: Electa Napoli / Edizioni La Conchiglia, 1994.

Capecchi, G. *Castelli parmigiani.* Parma: Artegrafica Silva, 1989.

Carpeggiani, P., and C. Tellini Perina. *Giulio Romano a Mantova.* Mantua: Sintesi, 1987.

Cassarono, E. *La villa medicea di Artimino.* Florence: Becocci, 1990.

Cazzato, V., and A. Mantovano. *Paradisi dell'eclettismo: Ville e villeggiature nel Salento.* Cavallino di Lecce: Capone, 1992.

Cevese, R. *Ville della provincia di Vicenza.* Milan: Rusconi, 1971.

Ciorli, R. *Le ville di Montenero.* Livorno: Il Gabbiano, n.d.

———. *Livorno: Storia di ville e palazzi.* Ospedaletto (Pisa): Pacini, 1994.

Conti, E. *Ville venete.* Novara: De Agostini, 1988.

Corti e dimore del contado mantovano. Florence: Vallecchi, 1969.

Cresti, C. *Civiltà delle ville toscane.* Udine: Magnus, 1992.

Cuppini, G., and A. M. Matteucci. *Ville del bolognese.* Bologna: Zanichelli, 1969.

———. *Ville del Bolognese.* Bologna: Zanichelli, 1988.

De Seta, C., L. Di Mauro, and M. Perone. *Ville vesuviane.* Milan: Rusconi, 1980.

Faganello, F. *Castelli del Trentino.* Ivrea: Priuli e Verlucca, 1993.

Farri, S. *Castelli reggiani.* Reggio Emilia: Bizzochi, 1981.

Ferrante, R., P. Da Re, and P. Orlandi. *Ville patrizie bergamasche.* Bergamo, Grafica & Arte, 1989.

Foschi, U. *Antiche ville della provincia di Forlì.* Forlì: Ente Provinciale per il Turismo, 1978.

Giusti, M. A. *Le ville segrete di Forte dei Marmi.* Milan: Electa, 1990.

———. *Villa Paolina a Viareggio e le dimore napoleoniche nel principato di Lucca.* Lucca: Pacini Fazzi, 1996.

Gobbi, G. *La villa fiorentina.* Florence: Uniedit, 1980.

Guaita, O. *Le ville della Lombardia.* Milan: Electa, 1994.

———. *Le ville della Toscana.* Rome: Newton & Compton, 1997.

———. *Le ville di Firenze.* Rome: Newton & Compton, 1996.

———. *Ville e giardini storici in Italia.* Milan: Electa, 1995.

Guerri, G. *Torri e castelli della provincia di Grosseto.* Grotte di Castro: Nuova Immagine, 1990.

Guidi, A. L. *Masserie e vecchi manieri nel Siracusano.* Palermo: Lombardi, 1990.

Hoffmann, P. *Le ville di Roma e dei dintorni.* Rome: Newton & Compton, 2001.

I castelli del Senese. Milan: Electa, 1985.

I castelli del territorio casentinese. Florence: Arnaud, 1990.

Langé, S. *Ville delle province di Como, Sondrio e Varese.* Milan: Sisar, 1968.

Langé, S., and F. Vitali. *Ville della provincia di Varese.* Milan: Rusconi, 1984.

Lauritzen, P., and R. Wolf. *Ville venete.* Milan: Mondadori, 2001.

Le ville nel paesaggio prealpino della provincia di Belluno. Milan: Charta, 1998.

Lensi Orlandi, G. L. *Le ville di Firenze.* Florence: Vallecchi, 1978.

Marton, G. P., M. Muraru, and J. Ackerman. *Civiltà delle ville venete.* Udine: Magnus, 1986.

Matteucci, A. M., C. E. Manfredi, and A. Coccioli Mastroviti. *Ville piacentine.* Piacenza: Tep, 1991.

Mavian, L. *Ville venete: Bibliografia.* Venice: Marsilio, 2001.

Mazzotti, G. *Le ville venete.* Treviso: Canova, 1987.

Medri, L. *La villa di Poggio a Caiano.* Florence: Becocci, 1998.

Merlini, L. *Ville e castelli.* Florence: Passigli, 1990.

Mongello, L. *Masserie di Puglia.* Bari: Adda, 1989.

Monicelli, F. *Ville e corti lungo il corso del Mincio.* Genoa: De Ferrari, 2001.

Motta, P. *Le ville di Genova.* Genoa: Sagep, 1986.

Nicolini, D. *La corte rurale nel Mantovano.* Milan: Silvana Editoriale, 1984.

Orlandi, P., and C. Perogalli. *Ville in Lombardia.* Milan: Celip, 1994.

Palazzi e ville del contado mantovano. Florence: Vallecchi, 1966.

Palvarini, M. R., and C. Perogalli. *Castelli dei Gonzaga.* Milan: Rusconi, 1983.

Pellegri, M. *Colorno: Villa ducale.* Parma: Artegrafica Silva, 1981.

Perogalli, C., and P. Favole. *Ville dei Navigli Lombardi.* Milan: Rusconi, 1982.

Perogalli, C., M. G. Sandri, and L. Roncai. *Ville delle province di Cremona e Mantova.* Milan: Rusconi, 1981.

Perogalli, C., M. G. Sandri, and V. Zanella. *Ville dell provincia di Brescia.* Milan: Rusconi, 1985.

———. *Ville della provincia di Bergamo.* Milan: Rusconi, 1983.

Pirondini, M. *Ducale palazzo di Sassuolo.* Genoa: Spiga, 1982.

Puppi, L., and G. C. Sciolla. *Le grandi ville italiane: Veneto, Toscana, Lazio.* Novara: De Agostini, 1998.

Rathschuler, A. *Andar per castelli nell'Alto Monferrato.* Genoa: Sagep, 1991.

Roggero Bardelli, B., M. G. Vinardi, and V. Defabiani. *Ville sabaude.* Milan: Rusconi, 1990.

Ronc, M. C., and D. Camisasca. *Castelli: Un viaggio fra le antiche dimore della Valle d'Aosta.* Quart: Musumeci, 1991.

Rossi Gribaudi, E. *Cascine e ville della pianura torinese.* Turin: Gribaudi, 1989.

———. *Vigne e ville della collina torinese.* Turin: Gribaudi, 1992.

San Pietro, S., and P. Gallo. *Villas in Italy and Canton Ticino.* Milan: L'Archivolto, 2001.

Scarpari, G. *Le ville venete.* Rome: Newton & Compton, 1980.

Scotti, G., M. Furlani Marchi, and V.Tentori. *Ville a Lecco e nella sua provincia.* Lecco: Periplo, 1992.

Sias, M. *Villini di Cagliari: Forma urbana dell'architettura borghese.* Cagliari: Coedisar, 2000.

Tomasi Lanza, G. *Dimore di Sicilia.* Venice: Arsenale, 1998.

Trotta, G. *Villa Strozzi "al boschetto."* Florence: Messaggerie Toscane, 1990.

———. *Ville fiorentine dell'Ottocento.* Florence: Becocci/Scala, 1994.

Ulmer, A. *Ville friulane: Storia e civiltà.* Udine: Magnus, 1993.

Ville e giardini d'Italia. Milan: Touring Club Italiano, 1997.

Ville e palazzi storici a San Cesario sul Panaro, Castelfranco Emilia, Nonantola. Nonantola: Centro Studi Storici Nonantolani, 2000.

Ville venete nel territorio di Mirano. Venice: Marsilio, 2001.

Ville venete: Catalogo e atlante del Veneto. Venice: Marsilio, 1996.

Ville venete: La provincia di Treviso. Venice: Marsilio, 2001.

Vincenti, A. *Ville della provincia di Novara.* Milan: Rusconi, 1988.

Warton, E. *Ville italiane e loro giardini.* Florence: Passigli, 1986.

Wuncham, M., T. Pape, and P. Marton. *Anddrea Palladio, 1508–1580: Un architetto tra Rinascimento e Barocco.* Cologne: Taschen, 1990.

Zangheri, L. *Ville della provincia di Firenze: La città.* Vol. 1. Milan: Rusconi, 1989.

Zoppé, L. *Ville del Friuli e della Venezia Giulia.* Udine: Itinera, 2001.

PLACES TO VISIT

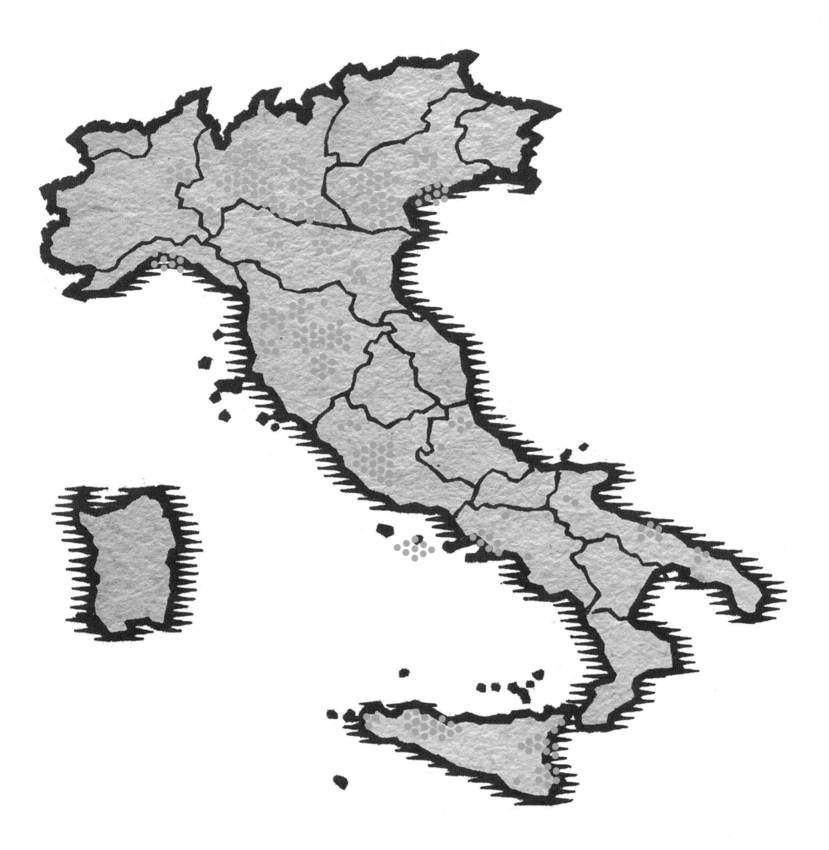

PIEDMONT

Province of Novara
Isola Bella, Stresa, 17th century, ○
Isola Madre, Stresa, 16th century, ○
Faraggiana, Meina, 19th century, ○
Pallavicino, Stresa, 19th century, ○
Ducale, Stresa, 18th century, ○
Taranto, Pallanza, 19th century, ○

LIGURIA

Province of Genoa
Duchessa di Galliera, Voltri, 17th century, ○
Gaslini, Genoa, 10th century, ◆
Grüber, Genoa, 18th century, ○
Luxoro, Nervi, 20th century ◆
Cambiaso, Genoa, 16th century, ○
Imperiale Scassi, Genoa 16th century
Pallavicini, Genoa, 19th century, ○
Imperiale di Sant'Angelo, Terralba, 16th century
Doria Pamphili, Genoa, 16th century, ○

LOMBARDY

Province of Sondrio
Vertemate Franchi, Piuro, 16th century, ○

Province of Como
Giovio, Como, 18th century, ◆
Rotonda, Inverigo, 19th century
Amalia, Erba, 18th century
Carlotta, Tremezzo, 19th century, ○
Melzi d'Eril, Bellagio, 19th century, ○
d'Este, Cernobbio, 16th century, ○
Belgioioso, Merate, 18th century, ○
Olmo, Como, 18th century, ○

Province of Varese
Cicogna Mozzoni, Bisuschio, 16th century, ○
Estense, Varese, 18th century, ○

Province of Milan
Arconti, Bollate, 18th century
Alari Visconti, Cernusco sul Naviglio, 18th century, ◆

Cavazzi della Somaglia, Orio Litta, 18th century
La Cazzola, Arcore, 17th century
Brentano, Corbetta, 18th century
Reale, monza, 18th century, ○
di Corbetta, Corbetta, 18th century, ◆
Antona Traversi, Meda 18th century
Borromeo d'Adda, Cassano d'Adda, 18th century, ○
Archinto, Robecco sul Naviglio, 18th century, ◆
Belgioioso, Milan, 18th century, ○
Visconti Maineri, Cassinetta di Lugagnano, 18th century
Litta, Lainate, 17th century

Province of Pavia
Pegazzera, Montalto, 18th century
Castello, Chignolo Po, 12th–18th century, ◆

Province of Bergamo
Terzi, Trescore Balneario, 18th century, ○
Mapelli, Ponte San Pietro, 18th century
Zanchi Antona Traversi, Mapello, 17th century
Pesenti, Paladina, 18th century
Suardi, Trescore Balneario, 19th century
Visconti Citterio, Brignano Gera d'Adda, 16th–17th century, ◆

Province of Brescia
Fenaroli, Rezzato, 18th century, ◆
Mazzucchelli, Mazzano, 18th century, ◆
Bettoni, Bogliaco in Gargnano, 16th century, ◆

Province of Cremona
Ala Ponzone, Sospiro, 19th century, ◆
Castello manfredi, Cicognolo, 19th century, ◆
Mina della Scala, Casteldidone, 16th century, ○
Medici del Vascello, San Giovanni in Croce, 16th century
Vimercati Sanseverino, Vaiano Cremasco, 17th century

Province of Pavia
Pegazzera, Montalto, 18th century

Castello, Chignolo Po, 12th–18th century, ◆

Province of Mantua
Castello di Bosco Fontana, Marmirolo, 16th century, ○
Ghirardina, Motteggiana, 15th century, ◆
L'Arrigona, S. Giacomo delle Segnate, 17th century, ◆
La Favorita, Porto Mantovano, 17th century, ○
Strozzi, Begozzo, 18th century, ○
Palazzo del Te, Mantua, 16th century, ○
Corte Cappelletta, Palidano, 16th–18th century, ◆

VENETO

Province of Verona
Allegri, Grezzano, 17th century, ○
Bertoldi, Negrar, 15th century, ○
Palazzo Giusti, Verona, 16th century, ○

Province of Vicenza
Loschi Zileri dal Verme, Monteviale, 18th century
Da Porto, Thiene, 15th century, ○
Godi, Lonedo di Lugo, 16th century, ○
La Rotonda, Vicenza, 16th century, ○
Piovene, Lonedo di Lugo, 16th century, ○
Pisani, Lonigo, 16th century, ○
Caldogno, Caldogno, 15th century, ○
Cordellina, Montecchio Maggiore, 18th century, ○
Barbarigo, Noventa, 16th century, ○
Valmarana "ai nani," Vicenza, 17th century, ○
Trissino Marzotto, Trissino, 18th century, ○

Province of Padua
Villa Pesaro, Este, 18th century
Corner, Carmignano di Brenta, 17th century, ○
Contarini, Piazzola sul Brenta, 17th century, ○
Molin, Mandriola, 16th century, ○
Emo Capodilista, Fanzolo, 16th century, ○
Barbarigo, Valsanzibio, 17th century, ○
Widman, Mira, 17th century, ○

CASTELLO DI CATAJO, Battaglia Terme,
   15th century, ○

Province of Venice
FOSCARINI, Stra, 17th century, ♦
TRON, Dolo, 18th century
FREGNANA , Fiesso d'Artico
FARSETTI, San Maria di Sala, 18th century, ○
RECANATI ZUCCONI, Fiesso d'Artico,
   17th century, ○
PRIULI, Venice, 17th century, ○
SORANZA, Fiesso d'Artico, 16th century, ○
PISANI, Stra, 18th century, ○
LA MALCONTENTA, Mira, 16th century, ○

Province of Treviso
LOREDAN, Venegazzù, 16th century, ○
DELLE ROSE, Treviso, 19th century, ♦
GIUSTINIAN, Roncade, 15th century, ○
BARBARO, Maser, 16th century, ○
AL PARADISO, Castelfranco Veneto,
   17th century
SPINEDA, Venegazzù

Province of Rovigo
LA BADOERA, Fratta Polesine, 16th century, ○
MOROSINI, Fiesso Umbertino, 18th century, ○
NANI MOCENIGO, Canda,
   16th–17th century, ○

EMILIA–ROMAGNA

Province of Parma
DUCALE , Colorno, 18th century, ○
ROCCA SANVITALE, Fontanellato,
   15th century, ○
DUCALE , Parma, 18th century, ○

Province of Modena
MANODORI, Castelnuovo Rangone,
   18th century
DUCALE, Sassuolo, 17th century, ○
PIO, Carpi, 15th century, ○
GIOVANARDI, Casinalbo, 18th century

Province of Bologna
ALDROVANDI, Chiesa Nuova, 18th century, ○
ROSSI, Pontecchio, 15th century, ♦

ALDINI, Bologna, 19th century, ♦
CASTELLO, Soversano, San Martino,
   14th–19th century, ♦
PEPOLI, Crevalcore, 15th century, ♦

TUSCANY

Province of Lucca
BANCALARI, Marlia, 16th century, ♦
COLFRANCO, San Martino in Freddana,
   16th century, ♦
REALE, Marlia, 19th century, ○
DEL VESCOVO, Marlia, 16th century, ○
MANSI, Segromigno, 17th century, ○
TORRIGIANI, Camigliano, 18th century, ○

Province of Pisa
AGOSTINI VENEROSI, San Giuliano Terme,
   17th century, ○
RONCIONI, San Giuliano Terme,
   16th–18th century
MEDICI , Camugliano, 16th–17th century
MEDICI, Coltano, 16th century, ♦

Province of Prato
MEDICI DI ARTIMINO "La Ferdinanda," Prato,
   16th century, ○

Province of Pistoia
DELLA COLONNA, Pontelungo, 18th century, ♦
ROSPIGLIOSI, Lamporecchio, 17th century, ○
GUARDATOIA, Pescia, 17th century
IMBARCATI, Pontenuovo, 16th–17th century
GARZONI, Collodi, 17th century, ○

Province of Florence
DI MONTALTO, Fiesole, 19th century, ○
IL CHIUSO, Florence, 17th century
PALAZZO BUDINI GATTAI, Florence,
   17th century, ○
LA GALLINA, Florence, 19th century
LE MASCHERE, Barberino del Mugello,
   17th century, ○
CASTELLO DI MUGNANA, Greve in Chianti,
   16th century, ○
MEDICI DI CAREGGI, Florence, 15th century
MEDICI , Poggio a Caiano, 16th century, ○
MEDICI , Castello, 16th century, ○

MEDICI "LA PETRAIA," Florence,
   16th century, ○
LA GAMBERAIA, Settignano, 17th–20th
   century, ○
MEDICI , Pratolino, 16th–19th century, ○
CORSI, Sesto Fiorentino, 17th century, ○
CORSINI, Castello, 17th century, ♦
MEDICI , Poggio Imperiale, Florence, 17th
   century, ○
UZZANO, Greve in Chianti, 17th century, ○
MEDICI , Castello del Trebbio, San Piero a
   Sieve, 15th century, ○
MEDICI , Cafaggiolo S. Piero a Sieve,
   15th century, ○

Province of Siena
DI CELSA, Sovicille, 14th–16th century
SANTA COLOMBA, Monterrigioni, Siena,
   16th century
CHIGI, Le Volte Alte, 16th century, ○
FONTERUTOLI, Castellina in Chianti,
   15th–20th century, ○
DI SELVOLA, Castelnuovo Berardenga,
   18th century
DI SOVICILLE, Sovicille, 14th –16th century, ♦
DI CETINALE, Sovicille, 17th century, ○

LATIUM

Province of Viterbo
FARNESE, Caprarola, 16th century, ○
SACRO BOSCO, Bomarzo, 16th century, ○
GIUSTINIANI, Bassano di Sutri

Province of Rome
DORIA PAMPHILI, Rome, 17th century, ○
GIULIA, Rome, 16th century, ○
FARNESINA, Rome, 16th century, ○
MEDICI , Rome, 16th century, ○
BORGHESE, Rome, 17th–18th century, ○
COLONNA, Rome, 18th century
MADAMA, Rome, 16th century, ♦
CORSINI, Rome, 16th –18th century, ♦
SACCHETTI CHIGI, Castel Fusano, 17th century
SANTACROCE, Oriolo Romano, 18th century
ALDOBRANDINI, Frascati, 17th century, ○
LANCELLOTTI, Frascati, 16th–19th century
LUDOVISI, Frascati, 16th–17th century, ○

MONDRAGONE, Frascati, 16th–17th century
GRAZIOLI, Frascati, 16th century, ○
LUDOVISI, Frascati, 16th–17th century, ◆
MATTEI, Marino, 16th–17th century
D'ESTE, Tivoli, 16th–19th century, ○

ABRUZZI

Province of Aquila
LA CITADELLA, L'Aquila, 16th century, ○
CASTELLO LAZZARONI, Gagliano Aterno,
 19th century, ○
CASTELLO PICCOLOMINI, Balsorano,
 15th century, ○
CASTELLO, Navelli, 14th century, ○

Province of Teramo
IL PINETO, Teramo, 20th century, ◆

CAMPANIA

Province of Caserta
REALE, Caserta, 18th century, ○

Province of Salerno
RUFOLO, Ravello, 13th century, ○

Province of Naples
DEI PAPIRI, Herculaneum, 1st century A.D.
CAMPOLIETO, Herculaneum, 18th century, ○
BIFULCO, Terzigno, 18th century, ◆
FIGLIUOLA, S. Sebastiano, 17th–18th
 century, ◆
BUONO, Portici, 18th century, ◆
REALE, Portici, 18th–19th century, ○
MANDRIANI, Portici, 18th century, ◆

CAPRI

Capri
DAMECUTA, Capri, 19th century, ◆
JOVIS, Capri, 1st century A.D., ○
MALAPARTE, Punto Fasullo, 20th century, ○
MATERITA, Capri, 19th century
SOLITARIA, Capri, 19th century, ◆

FAINARDI, Capri, 19th century, ◆

Anacapri
CASA ROSSA, Anacapri, 19th century, ○
FERSEN, Anacapri, 19th century
SAN MICHELE, Anacapri, 19th century, ○

APULIA

Province of Foggia
LA TORRETTA, San Severo, 19th century, ◆
PALMIERI, Sannicandro, 17th century, ◆

Province of Bari
MONTEROSSO, Monopoli, 17th century, ○
CASTELLO MARCHIONE, Conversano,
 17th century
CONCHIA, Monopoli, 17th–18th century
PALAZZO PELLICCIARI, Gravina, 18th century
CARAMANNA, Monopoli, 17th century, ◆
SANTISSIMA, Turi, 19th century, ◆

Province of Brindisi
SAN MARCO, Fasano, 17th century
SAN DOMENICO, Savelletri di Fasano,
 18th century, ○
CARESTIA, Ostuni, 18th century

Province of Taranto
LEVRANO D'AQUINO, Taranto, 18th century, ◆

SICILY

Province of Trapani
TORRE DORIA, Castellammare, 14th century, ◆
SAFINA, Castellammare, 20th century
ELENA, Valderice, 20th century

Province of Palermo
WHITAKER, Palermo, 19th century, ○
CHINESE VILLA, Palermo, 19th century, ○
DE CORDOVA, Palermo, 18th century, ◆
TERRASI, Palermo, 18th century, ◆
MERCADANTE, Palermo, 18th century, ◆
BONOCORE, Palermo, 18th century, ◆
PANTELLERIA, Palermo, 18th century, ◆

LA FAVORITA, Palermo, 19th century, ○
PARTANNA, Palermo, 18th century, ◆
SPINA, Palermo, 18th century, ◆
TRAVIA, Bagheria, 18th century, ○
PALAGONIA, Bagheria. 18th century, ○
VALGUARNERA, Bagheria, 18th century
SPEDALOTTO, Bagheria, 19th century, ◆
BUFERA, Bagheria, 17th century, ◆
RAMACCA, Bagheria, 18th century, ◆

Province of Ragusa
CASTELLO, Donnafugata, 19th century, ○

Province of Messina
ROBERTO, Messina, 20th century
BOSURCI, Messina, 17th century, ◆

Province of Catania
MONTE D'ORO, Catania, 20th century
POLITINI, Catania, 17th century, ◆
DI BELLA, Catania, 20th century, ◆
MARGHERITA, Catania, 20th century, ◆
CUTORE, Catania, 19th century, ◆
MODICA, Catania, 20th century, ◆
TRIGONA, Catania, 20th century, ◆
VECCHIO, Catania, 19th century, ◆
PENNISI DI FLORISTELLA, Acireale, 19th
century, ◆

Province of Siracusa
TORRE MILOCCA, Montalto, 18th century
TAFURI, Portopalo, 19th century, ○
TORRE LANDOLINA, Isola, 18th century
TORRE CUBBA, Santa Teresa, 16th–19th century
MASSERIA TREMILIA, Tremilia, 19th century
ITALIA, Isola, 19th century, ◆
ELEONORA DI VILLADORATA, Noto Marina,
 17th century, ◆

LEGEND
○ : Open to the public
◆ : Exterior views from nearby
The other villas listed here may be viewed
only from afar.

INDEX OF VILLAS

INDEX OF NAMES AND PLACES

CAPTIONS, PAGES 298/299

The balcony overlooking the drawing room of the Villa Strozzi in Begozzo (Mantua).

PHOTOGRAPHIC CREDITS

pp. 18, 19, 208:
Luciano Pedicini, Naples

pp. 4, 5: A. Bertarelli Collection of Prints and Engravings, Milan

Entries in the index relate to the text only.